A call for connection

solutions for creating
a *whole* new culture

Gail Bernice Holland

NEW WORLD LIBRARY
NOVATO, CALIFORNIA

New World Library
14 Pamaron Way
Novato, CA 94949

Cover design: Bill Stanton
Cover illustration: Bonnie Rieser
Text design: Aaron Kenedi

Library of Congress Cataloging-in-Publication Data

Holland, Gail Bernice, 1940–
    A call for connection : solutions for creating a whole new culture /
  by Gail Bernice Holland.
        p.   cm.
    Includes bibliographical references.
    ISBN 1-57731-039-X (pbk. : alk. paper)
    1. Ethical problems. 2. Social problems. I. Title.
  BJ1031.H75   1998   98-14114
  303.48'4—dc21   CIP

First printing, June 1998
Printed in Canada on acid-free paper
ISBN 1-57731-039-X
Distributed to the trade by Publishers Group West

10 9 8 7 6 5 4 3 2 1

To my beloved daughter, Anya Bernice Holland.
This book is written with the hope of building
a better future for your generation and
all generations that follow.

CONTENTS

ACKNOWLEDGMENTS

I am grateful to the Institute of Noetic Sciences (IONS) for their financial help when I first began writing this book. I now work for the Institute as editor of the magazine *Connections* but several years ago, when IONS provided the initial support for my book, I was an independent journalist, and their assistance allowed me to start my research. I particularly want to thank Winston Franklin, IONS president, whose commitment to this book sustained me through the inevitable difficult moments of a long-term project.

To write a book covering so many different fields, I had to interview hundreds of people. Although many names are mentioned in these chapters, I couldn't include comments from all the individuals who provided me with information over the years, but I want to stress that I am indebted to everyone who took the time to tell me about the new developments benefiting society.

I also want to thank my friends who offered encouragement and love during the whole process: Marcy Bachmann, Heather and Jim Barry, Carolyn Dobervich, Shirley Lewis Harris, Susan Hoebich, Sewellyn Kaplan, Ann Keen, Rosalie Malec, Joan Tharp, Lynn Thomas, Eleanor Tomic, and Anne Weinberger.

It was a pleasure to work with my editor, Jason Gardner. His insightful comments and editing skills made the final work on this book a joy.

Thank you also to Bill Stanton, Bonnie Rieser, and Aaron Kenedi for the beautiful cover.

Toward Wholeness: Connecting the Heart, Conscience, and Spirit

While working as a geologist in the Alaskan wilds, Cynthia Dusel-Bacon's arms were eaten by a bear. A helicopter had dropped her off in a remote area to do geologic field mapping for the U.S. Geological Survey. Cynthia was working alone, enjoying the solitude and beauty of the wilderness, when suddenly a female black bear appeared out of the brush. Cynthia never determined whether the bear was defending its cub, or whether she had startled it, but the result was the same: For the next hour she became a rag doll in the bear's mouth. The bear clawed her, chewed her, dragged her over rocks.

Cynthia stayed alive by maintaining her composure. When the

bear paused for a few minutes, she pulled her walkie-talkie from her rucksack and with amazing calmness contacted the helicopter pilot: "Ed, this is Cynthia. Come quickly. I'm being eaten by a bear."

As she described her location, the bear attacked again. Fortunately, the helicopter pilot heard her call for help. She was rescued and rushed to a hospital. Her arms were severely damaged, however, and the doctors had no choice but to amputate them both.

Cynthia had to learn how to dress herself, feed herself, *live* with herself all over again. During her rehabilitation, she rebuilt not only her physical strength but her inner strength. She had the courage and the spirit to turn bitterness into something better. Her friends and family watched with pride as she mastered the art of operating a can opener with her feet, learned how to grab a milk carton with her teeth, and eventually, equipped with prosthetic devices, returned to work. Cynthia is now married and has a son. She will tell you that you don't need arms to give love to a child. Over the years she has helped other amputees appreciate that as long as the human spirit and heart are active, you can always be whole.

This book's prime focus is wholeness. It explores how schools, businesses, our health care system — all segments of society — have begun to adopt a whole systems approach, specifically fostering the best in human nature in order to create a more unified, compassionate way of life. To write this book, I have spent several years examining these positive changes. You might wonder why I would start the first chapter with a story about one woman and how she overcame personal tragedy. What is the connection between Cynthia's personal struggle and the larger question of how we can improve society?

As a writer who has worked for both newspapers and magazines, I am acutely aware that the media are often criticized for its constant barrage of bad news. Yet the media do report good news, not necessarily on page one, but most local newspapers run occasional features about organizations tackling societal problems. Cynthia Dusel-Bacon's story of courage is an even more common example of "good news" about individuals who demonstrate the immense inner resources of the human being. Indeed, I have observed that readers pay more attention to personal stories about people who overcome hardships than news about small gains in solving social problems. To me, this is the irony: Cynthia wrestled with a bear, and we can draw the analogy that society is also being torn apart as it struggles with tremendous difficulties. But although we may root for Cynthia to persevere, too many of us resign ourselves to the belief that is impossible to improve the larger human condition. We tend to take our problems for granted, to greet solutions to social problems with open skepticism. We are overwhelmed with the magnitude of difficult issues that need to be addressed, and many people assume that successes in local programs have little impact on a national or international level.

I would like to counter this negativity. The intent of this book is to deliver hope and inspiration in a realistic package for readers who want to find out not only what might be done in the future to improve society but what *is* being done right now to create a better way of life.

People know the ugly side of human nature. We want to be shown beauty, what we can be. Good news isn't an escape from reality; it's the best way to improve reality. When we read about effective programs, we can replicate them. When we learn about ideas that could change life for the better, we can take action. When we hear about individuals who make a difference, we're inspired.

Consider this book a jigsaw puzzle. The following chapters offer bits and pieces of information about to how to improve our personal and professional lives, how to prevent environmental

disasters, discourage corporate greed, and overhaul the educational and economic systems. I invite you, the reader, to fit these
different reforms together so you can see the big picture.
Individually, each reform appears to have a minor effect, but the
impact of the collective changes is enormous. I believe they are
shaping a whole new culture.

When I began my research for this book I was trying to find
solutions to apparently separate social problems. I was surprised to
discover a connection between these solutions. It is this connection that is creating the new culture. Initially, the current changes
in medicine seem far removed from the reforms being proposed in
schools, but in both areas the emphasis is now on taking care of
the *whole* person — mind, body, and spirit.

During my interviews with hundreds of people from all disciplines, the theme of wholeness kept surfacing over and over again.
Nearly everyone complained that society has become too fragmented and compartmentalized. Each group formed to tackle a
specific problem — be it the ozone layer, unemployment, or overpopulation — finds itself in the position of having to compete
against other groups for financial backing and public attention. In
particular, people dwelt on what society lacks. They are disturbed
about how the proliferation of special-interest groups cause profits
to routinely come before principles. What is missing, they say, is a
social conscience. What is missing from schools where students
cheat on exams, and sell drugs in hallways, is explicit guidance
toward social and moral development. In a society where child
abuse hides behind family walls, and the bodies of the homeless
block sidewalks, we're missing the firm safety net that compassion
brings. Missing from the disciplines of both science and medicine
is a complete composite of the human experience. Science too
often ignores the spiritual dimension of life, while the mechanistic
model of medicine treats the body as a machine without a heart.

And let us not forget the arts. But whenever budgets are tight, the arts are quickly forgotten.

Missing in too many places is the best of humanity: our heart, conscience, and spirit. People feel society's increasing preoccupation with materialism is undermining our more noble values. A growing consensus says that we can't alleviate the social ills of this world by relying on more laws or more money. They are not enough. We are at last acknowledging that our problems can only be solved if we ward off the worst in human nature by aggressively cultivating the best in us. Thus we see a call for connection — a connection not just between the different segments of our lives, but even more important, a call to reconnect with the best in human nature. We're crying out for wholeness; we're desperately trying to return the missing parts — the heart, human spirit, and conscience — to all areas of our lives.

Still, aiming for the best in us is obviously not a new quest. Great leaders and religious traditions have always tried to guide us toward justice and compassion. So why is today different? Maybe it is because we are fed up with the politics of negativity and divisiveness. Maybe it is because we are recognizing that violence, poverty, or drug abuse don't develop out of the blue; they result, in part, from seeing red! In short, anger, greed, and other human faults are the direct cause of each social crisis. Yet, by the same reasoning, we can also solve these problems. We just need the intent.

The question becomes, how do you transfer talk to action? How do you achieve idealistic goals in a way that is practical, effective, and nonthreatening to the general public, especially when goals and principles of this nature can easily be manipulated and misconstrued?

Modern research is coming to our rescue. The latest scientific findings are confirming the critical role the human spirit and heart both play in how we learn and how we heal. As a result, we have already started to restructure schools and medical care to foster, rather than neglect, our finer qualities.

In many ways, whole-person medicine is transforming not just medicine but science itself. Rustum Roy, one of the leading material scientists in the United States, notes that for the last 500 years science was a slave to the reductionist model — the idea that the whole is merely the sum of its parts. However, as a scientist, he watched new ways of thinking in health topple the reductionist stranglehold on how we perceive life. Within the last few years, he says, millions of people have experimented with holistic healing therapies because they realize, through direct personal experience, that you can't treat the body without treating the mind and spirit. "What is happening is utterly profound," Roy told me. "These millions of individuals now know whole-person medicine works."

If reductionist medicine is on the way out, he adds, then so is reductionist science. People are now beginning to adopt a whole-systems approach to all disciplines, all reality.

The present search for solutions, with its emphasis on wholeness, is spiritual in nature, but the shift in values is not tied to any specific religion or political party. I stress this point because the concern has always been how to prevent one group of people from imposing their perception of morality and spirituality on everyone else. On the other hand, spirituality in its purest form is more about a way of being than a set of beliefs. The distinction is significant. Such qualities as compassion, love, and integrity are universal; they say more about how we live than what religion we follow.

The most encouraging news of all is that idealism is being expressed through pragmatic reforms. Business leaders, educators, and individuals from all parts of society are finding effective and practical ways to convert higher principles into direct action.

The cultural shift in values that I document in the following pages is being verified by the experts who track future trends.

Duane Elgin, a social scientist, leader of the voluntary simplicity movement, and director of the nonprofit organization Choosing Our Future, examined some of the major United States and global surveys conducted in the past decade. He found that a worldwide change in perceptions and priorities is emerging. This new social pattern and global paradigm, he says, stems from a "whole-systems view of things — one that is intensely concerned with relationships of all kinds, including the ecological, social, and spiritual well-being of all humankind."

For instance, Elgin refers to a "World Values Survey," representing nearly 70 percent of the world's population, which revealed that "despite the economic problems in many areas of the world, majorities in most of the twenty-four nations surveyed gave environmental protection a higher priority than economic growth."

Environmental problems also demand a whole-systems approach, but as Elgin emphasizes, the solutions require not just practical changes but a shift in attitudes. The depletion of natural resources is forcing us to recognize we can't continue chasing materialistic goals. As people begin to simplify their lives, the survey experts are noticing that they are replacing the need to buy possessions with the need to develop a lifestyle that provides a greater sense of personal well-being. This change often leads to a reappraisal of social values.

In the United States, an extensive study conducted by sociologist Paul Ray identified a rapid rise of what he calls the Integral Culture. "Compared to the rest of society," says Ray, "the bearers of Integral Culture have values that are more idealistic and spiritual, have more concern for relationships and psychological development, are more environmentally concerned, and are more open to creating a positive future."

"According to my research," he continues, "this group comprises about 24 percent of the adults in the United States or about

44 million people. If indeed an Integral Culture is emerging, we are experiencing a very unusual time in history — for change in the dominant cultural pattern happens only once or twice a millennium." Ray also points out that this new subculture of 44 million people is "bigger than any comparable group seen at the birth of any previous societal renaissance."

Most people remain unaware of the extent of this cultural transformation because we're witnessing a gentle evolution in human consciousness, not a revolution based on dramatic acts. Yet everywhere one looks people are working on solutions to correct problems. In one corner the talk centers on how to prevent crime. Talk to others, and they highlight the movement toward sustainability. Throughout this book people promote other major movements, such as the interfaith movement or the movement to restructure health care or education. These movements may seem dissimilar but in the end each one represents a different finger on the same pair of hands trying to reshape the world.

Moreover, as we learn how our well-being is connected to love and the fullness of the human spirit, these lessons can be transferred to the workplace. The way we conduct business is connected to what we teach children, which is connected to the building blocks of science and the arts. In the long run, improving the individual and improving society are also intertwined. Environmental issues are tied to economic issues, and economic issues are tied to peace issues, and all these issues and dilemmas are inextricably tied to values — not dollar values but humanitarian values, which brings us back full circle.

Many of these new ways of thinking and acting, especially in medicine and business, have already been written about, but we keep looking at each subject in isolation. In this age of commercialism and sensationalism we expect *everything* to be "new" and "different" — but we don't have to keep reinventing the wheel.

President Clinton once talked about how difficult it is to persuade groups to replicate programs that work. "I consider it to be the major failure of my public life," Clinton said, "that every problem in our society today is being solved by somebody somewhere, and I can't get it to be replicated." His point is important: We may not have all the answers, but we do have some of the solutions.

As we move into the next century, many of us are reevaluating our purpose on this planet. It is about time — for many say time is running out unless we change our ways. Even the life of democracy is at stake. Czech President Vaclav Havel warns that democracy arouses mistrust in some parts of the world because it lacks a "spiritual dimension that connects all cultures and, in fact, all humanity."

"If democracy is to spread successfully throughout the world," Havel said on a visit to the United States, "and if civic coexistence and peace are to spread with it, then it must happen as part of an endeavor to find a new and genuinely universal articulation of that global human experience, which even we, western intellectuals, are once more beginning to recollect, one that connects us with the mythologies and religions of all cultures and opens for us a way to understand their values. It must expand simply as an environment in which we may all engage in a common quest for the general good."

The quest has begun in earnest. Pessimists may be correct that there is no magic formula for transformation, no absolute answers, flawless programs, or perfect individuals. Nevertheless, throughout society, legitimate guideposts are revealing the many paths we can take to move us *toward* unity. The paths may be different, but the solutions we're seeking in today's world share a common concern: no matter what the discipline, no matter what the goal, regardless of politics, or the desire to make a profit, we can no longer afford to ignore the crucial role of the heart, conscience, and human spirit in everything we pursue.

A new way of living lies within our grasp if we are prepared to recognize and understand how these positive piecemeal changes fit together, and how they can be emulated. Then we can detect the vigor of unbounded possibilities. Then we can create a world that is more whole, compassionate, and balanced. Enjoy the puzzle.

CHAPTER ONE

Building a Connection between Spirituality and Science

The divisions are distinct: There is the officially sanctioned separation between church and state. And then there is the unofficial but society-approved separation between religion and science. By nature, religion is subjective, a private experience based on personal beliefs. By design, science is objective, a public enterprise based on controlled experiments. We humans straddle these two powerful frames of reference, which profoundly influence our lives and yet which operate as if they have nothing in common. Before we can begin to comprehend where the world is headed, we first need to acknowledge how religion and science have pulled us in opposite directions.

A priest who was interviewed for this book said defensively, "The world has to change, not religion." But the religious establishment cannot afford to miss the transformation rumbling across the planet. Religion has been derailed far too many times because the passenger list has been exclusionary. As we know too well, the divisions between religions have caused our most intractable wars and ripped nations and continents apart.

Science, too, has its own rigid boundaries. It has chiseled out a fragmented view of life based on a reductionistic, mechanistic model, with the world viewed as a giant machine of discrete parts. In this model, human consciousness is the material masterpiece, but its artistry is credited solely to the different parts of the physical brain. Thus the human spirit and any concept of divine purpose are considered scientifically irrelevant. Physical matter is ultimate. But science certainly has ignored some of the things that matter most.

In Western society we are inclined to worship scientific inventions but fear religious interventions. When seeking solutions to human problems — be it pollution, an international conflict, or heart disease — we rely more on technological fixes than spiritual solutions. We fear religion will cross over into places it doesn't belong, or where we worry it will do more harm than good. While the American separation between church and state is a necessary and appropriate safeguard, this compartmentalization has permeated our entire culture. In the workplace, the doctor's office, or at dinner with friends, we talk much more about the weather than the state of our souls.

Indeed, the repression of our internal world has created a lopsided materialistic culture far too dependent on outward goals for satisfaction. We are losing faith not only in a God, but in our government, our institutions — ourselves. From violence in the streets to a lack of ethics in the office, people agree that many of our problems stem from some social malaise, from some spiritual deficiency.

A NEW UNDERSTANDING OF SPIRITUALITY

Emerging as a direct response to this perilous imbalance is a shift in attitude toward spirituality. This shift isn't the work of a single leader or religion. It appears to be a spontaneous reaction to a spiritual crisis, each burst of activity seemingly isolated but subtly interrelated. We are also distinguishing between spirituality and religion. Most often, the word spirituality is now used as a universal term to describe the mystical core of innate goodness within the human being. The world's organized religions are viewed as the different wrappings around this core, with each religion promoting its own doctrines and practices. The reason for this differentiation is that even though there is an undeniable yearning in our chaotic world for greater moral leadership, and even though people claim they want a society with a soul, they worry about the steering capabilities of religious institutions and their dogmas.

One religious leader who understands these shifts is Methodist Bishop Melvin Talbert, who serves on the executive committee of the National Council of Churches of Christ, the largest ecumenical organization of Protestant and Orthodox Christians in the United States, representing nearly 51 million members. "I see a spiritual hunger on the part of so many people," Talbert says. "But at the same time these people are not desirous of immediately hooking up with institutionalized religion. I believe this is happening because they are not ready to claim all of the baggage that religious groups bring along, including the churches I lead. That doesn't deny the fact that they are spiritual beings and yearn for some kind of a spiritual relationship that affirms this side of their being."

Talbert views these attitudes as a positive trend rather than a negative one. He reminds us that in the '50s and '60s it was considered fashionable to go to church; it was a place to be seen and to socialize. Although there is nothing wrong with the church acting as a social gathering place, says Talbert, the spiritual quest was not always genuine. "I think in those days the church was in a sense *used*. From my perspective, people are joining churches and movements today because they truly want to be more in touch with their spiritual side. The church experience is changing. It is having to be more authentic."

People are also now freely crossing denominational lines, he adds, seeking real spiritual support wherever it is provided. Part of this search is for individual attention, not just an institutional experience. "They want us to help them understand what it means to be a spiritual person in this day and age and how it will impact them personally," he says. "I think the wave of the future is going to be a one-to-one relationship. Churches will have to focus on small groups where people can have this kind of intimate relationship, and that is something new for us."

When Bishop Talbert was president of the National Council of Churches he was invited to the White House to talk to President Clinton about national and international issues of social justice. Talbert is an African American who knew Reverend Martin Luther King, Jr., and like King, feels that spiritual leaders have a responsibility to *act* in order to alleviate societal problems.

However, he also carefully avoids the wall-building trap of *us* against *them*. If he has a political concern he talks to both Republicans and Democrats, and he emphasizes values that can be embraced by all religious people. Talbert counsels that it would be disastrous for a government to resemble, in any form, a theocratic organization.

People are understandably uncomfortable with the suggestion

that solutions to world problems might be spiritual. In the United States, the religious right wields its political muscle in one corner of the Republican party, but their do-it-my-way-or-else brand of morality scares others who realize how easily religious interests can manipulate politics. The entrance of spiritually directed ideas into world affairs demands constant caution to guard against just this sort of dogmatism and zealotry. We must now decide whether to confront this dilemma head-on, whether the role of religion on the world stage can, if approached wisely, be more constructive than destructive.

THE INTERFAITH MOVEMENT

Groups of people have often spoken about turning spirituality into a neutral force to serve the common good of the planet. But until this point, a united, global effort has been missing. This effort is now under way, triggered in part by the interfaith movement.

When we scrupulously follow the core teachings of the great wisdom traditions we are guided explicitly toward wholeness; the word "holy" itself is embedded in the word "whole." Even though historically political divisions have burgeoned under the name of religion, these divisions are human-made rather than divinely dictated, and today a massive undertaking is afoot to dismantle the barriers humans have erected over the centuries. On a personal level, women and homosexuals are asking that religions end all forms of sexism, racism, or homophobia. And on a more universal level, religious leaders are making serious attempts to reconcile theological differences. "Difference" remains a loaded word — loaded with hate and weapons, as people who worship other gods, or other ideas, attack one another. The most hopeful development to dissolve this divisiveness is a global interfaith movement.

Diana Eck, a professor of comparative religion and Indian

studies at Harvard University, who studies religious diversity, sees great promise in current interfaith overtures. At an interfaith conference held in San Francisco, she told the participants, "A careful observer of the world's religions today would have to report that not only is there a rise in religious chauvinism and funda-mentalism, but on the other side of the ledger there is also a new movement, a movement towards pluralism, a movement of interreligious dialogue, a movement of interfaith encounter, and when the history of the twentieth century comes to be written, this will surely be one of the most important movements of this century — a movement of people of various religious traditions deliberately setting out to meet one another."

The purpose of the interfaith movement is not to promote conformity or convert someone to another religion. The intent is to highlight commonality. Rigid disagreements between individu-als of different faiths will probably always exist, but it is easier to respect and cherish these differences if you can honor common principles. The interfaith groups hope that when people become willing to listen to each other, far fewer disagreements will turn deadly; "Dialogue or Die" is a slogan they have adopted to explain why this movement is so urgently needed.

Eck stresses that interreligious dialogue has become even more crucial in today's world because the global map of ethnicities and religions has been completely reshaped through the unprecedent-ed migration of millions of people. "London," she explains, "is now part of the Muslim world. Chicago is part of the Muslim world. We're still running to catch up with that reality."

Part of that reality, says Eck, is finding a way to live with one another that goes beyond mere tolerance. "If I tolerate you as a person of another faith I don't have to know anything about you. Tolerance does nothing to remove our ignorance of one another. Tolerance is simply too thin a foundation for the world of religious differences in which we now live."

What is required, she believes, is not just a passive acceptance of diversity but direct ways to actively elicit mutual understanding. Whereas the political and economic implications of today's interdependent world are rapidly being analyzed and turned to our advantage, until recently, little notice has been paid to the importance of building a global religious infrastructure.

WORKING FOR THE COMMON GOOD

Today, such an infrastructure is gradually being established. An international United Religions Initiative (URI) has been formed to actively encourage religions to work for the benefit of *all* people. This organization was inspired by the interfaith concept, and is patterned after the United Nations. The goal is to build a strong global forum where the great religions can meet on a regular basis, under an agreed-upon charter, to try to resolve difficult social issues.

Bishop William Swing, head of the Episcopal Diocese in California, conceived of URI. In the past, he says, the world's religions "spoke infrequently and had no permanent place, no regular sessions, no continuous search to enhance global good."

The initiative began in 1996, with fifty-five people from the various world religions. By 1998, membership had reached half a million people around the world. "At first," says Swing, "We didn't have a staff or office, and now we are growing so fast we had to leave our first building and get another one. Our goal is to reach 60 million people by the year 2000 and we think we're right on target."

URI branches are forming all over the world. When asked why URI is growing so rapidly, Bishop Swing answers, "There is an enormous backlog of frustration over the killing and hatred in the world done in the name of religion. Here is a story I can tell you: A man was riding on a train in Sri Lanka, and the man next to him was reading the literature from the United Religions Initiative. When the train stopped, the man said, 'May I have that literature because I would like to write to the Bishop in San Francisco and tell him my story?'

"So he sent me a letter and what he told me was that years ago he fell in love with a Buddhist woman. But he was a Christian and where he comes from the Buddhists hate the Christians. Both sets of parent forbade them to marry, but they went ahead and announced their wedding. The parents got together and poisoned the young couple; they believed death was better than a marriage.

"Fortunately, the couple were rushed to the hospital and lived. They went on to have the wedding, but at the ceremony a fight broke out between the families and three people died; two people had their eyes poked out.

"The man who wrote this letter then said, 'I had a deep conviction at my wedding years ago that there has to be a United Religions. So I started an organization to meet this need in Sri Lanka. I had no idea anybody out in the world was trying to do this globally. We now have 1,400 people in our organization. We're very poor, but we are yours.'"

"I get letters every day from people around the world," Bishop Swing adds. "But when you get a letter like that you know there is a purpose for a United Religions Initiative. It is going to work."

Their plan, he says, is to sign a United Religions charter in the year 2000. Although URI is based on the United Nations concept, Bishop Swing emphasizes one major organizational difference: "When the United Nations was formed, the only model for getting people together was to build a big building, and create a big bureaucracy around an assembly and security council. In the year 2000 we will be able to get people together technologically and through satellites on a daily, instantaneous basis, without having to go to one place, and without a huge bureaucracy."

Swing frankly admits that a United Religions is not a panacea, however. "I think it would be naive to think that this institution would solve all religious animosities," he says. "But this is the place from where we are going to struggle. We didn't even have a starting point until now. A United Religions is a symbol that religious people in the world actually believe that all of life does ultimately hold together and that a symbol of unity is worth striving for."

A GLOBAL ETHIC

The precedent for bringing people of different faiths together was set in 1893, when representatives from the various world faiths attempted to communicate with one another at the Parliament of the World's Religions in Chicago. One hundred years later, in 1993, the Parliament of the World's Religions convened again. Over eight thousand people from all over the world came together, this time knowing that more action needed to be taken. They accomplished one major achievement — an impressive 95 percent of the religious leaders who attended the conference signed a statement toward a declaration of a common global ethic. If taken seriously, this agreement could influence civilization far into the future.

It stated: "By a global ethic we do not mean a global ideology or a single unified religion beyond all existing religions, and certainly not the domination of one religion over all others. By a global ethic we mean a fundamental consensus of binding values, irrevocable standards, and personal attitudes. Without such a fundamental consensus on an ethic, sooner or later every community will be threatened by chaos or dictatorship, and individuals will despair."

Despair. These religious leaders were not trying to be melodramatic. There were only echoing what everyone sees and hears: increasing violence, social disarray, and economic disparity.

The concept of a global spiritual ethic may seem unrealistic when set against the bleak backdrop of these problems, but people have begun to concede that political or monetary solutions alone are not enough to provide lasting solutions. Building bigger weapons doesn't stop conflict, just as producing more food doesn't stop hunger. Joan Holmes, president of the Hunger Project, once made this plea: "Ending hunger is more than digging wells. It is more than planting crops. It is even more than feeding children. Ending hunger is about transforming the way we relate to other human beings."

In the 1990s more and more people are framing difficult issues in this context of ethics and spirituality. Gerald Barney is a founder and executive director of the Millennium Institute, an organization that helps nations prepare long-term plans for sustainable development and security. Barney's job is to look into the future. When in office, President Jimmy Carter asked Barney to conduct a Global 2000 report on the future of the world's environment, population, and economic development. Several years later Barney updated this report. In it, he cautioned: "Our definitions of progress and success must take into account the future well-being of the entire ecosphere, not just the human part of it. Such a changed understanding of progress and success will require a new understanding of humankind as a species, a new approach to the ethics of interspecies relations, and a new vision for the future of Earth."

The report underscored this conclusion: "The task before us is fundamentally spiritual in nature: to discover who we humans are, how we are to relate to each other and to the whole community of life, and what we are to do, individually and collectively, here on Earth."

A BRIDGE BETWEEN SPIRITUALITY AND SCIENCE

Yesterday when somebody said they were religious, few questions were asked. Today, we're admitting how little we know about spirituality and its role in our life. Most of us have acted as if everything we wanted to know about spirituality had already been said, had already been debated. Sir John Marks Templeton founded the John Templeton Foundation with the explicit purpose of encouraging more research on spirituality and the relationship between science and religion. He is opening the door to this unexplored terrain.

Templeton became a business legend in international money management and was knighted by Britain's Queen Elizabeth in recognition of his extensive philanthropy. Templeton has spent his life seeking intangible assets, not just material wealth. As a child he considered becoming a Christian missionary but over the years has refrained from attaching himself to one religion. His passion, instead, is to learn more about all religions.

"Throughout human history," he says, "every religion has tried to direct attention to ancient scriptures and prophets rather than searching for any new information."

When asked why we need more information, Templeton draws this analogy: "Let us suppose that medicine had adopted the attitude years ago that they didn't want to learn anything new. Your physical condition would be miserable today."

Currently, he explains, over $2 billion a day is spent on research in medicine and science. But very little is spent on spiritual progress. This is one reason why his foundation established the Templeton Prize for Progress in Religion. The prize is larger than any other award, including the Nobel Prize, and is awarded annually to any individual who advances humankind's understanding of religion and spirituality. Templeton's goal is to wake the world to our stagnation, and then spark interest in aggressively investigating this area of our lives. His foundation publishes a Who's Who in Theology and Science. A few years ago only about 600 scientists worldwide had published anything on spiritual subjects. Now there are over 1,000 scientists on the growing list.

Paul Davies, a British physicist and writer who lives in South Australia, is one of the recipients of the Templeton Prize. He is the author of over twenty books, including *The Mind of God* and *God and the New Physics*. In his acceptance speech for the prize, Davies talked about how the universe is structured in such a way that he personally believes there has to be meaning and purpose to existence. "Some of my colleagues embrace the same scientific facts as I, but deny any deeper significance. They shrug aside the breathtaking ingenuity of the laws of physics, the extraordinary felicity of nature, and the surprising intelligibility of the physical world, accepting these things as a package of marvels that just happens to be. But I cannot do this.

"Whatever the universe as a whole may be about," Davies continued, "the scientific evidence suggests that we, in some limited yet ultimately still profound way, are an integral part of its purpose."

Davies realizes that this line of reasoning raises difficult questions, the biggest one being: What is the nature of consciousness? If humans are not a meaningless by-product of a mechanistic universe, then how does our consciousness fit into the cosmic scheme? He admits, "We still haven't a clue how mind and matter are related, nor what process led to the emergence of mind from matter in the first place."

DOES CONSCIOUSNESS COME FIRST?

The new inquiry into the nature of the human mind is causing an earthquake within conventional science. As a result, a difficult but promising connection is being built between spirituality and science. In fact, scientists are now helping to reveal aspects of spirituality that have not been understood in the modern Western world, such as the connection between spirituality and our physical well-being. (See chapter 3.)

However, the most dramatic shift in thinking is due to the latest scientific findings that suggest physical matter might not be fundamental after all. Although most scientists still cling to the opinion that consciousness is derived from matter and is nothing more than a mechanical brain process, a small number are calling for an expansion of the scientific worldview by insisting consciousness cannot be reduced to brain function alone. The mechanistic, deterministic model of the universe has slid into obsolescence, but it is taking the scientific establishment, as well as the general public, a long time to fully understand this revolution and its spiritual implications.

Physicists, especially, have been influenced by the introduction of quantum mechanics. Certain aspects of quantum mechanics, such as Heisenberg's Uncertainty Principle and Bell's Theorem, have provoked vigorous discussion about the role of consciousness in shaping reality. Simply stated, in the late 1920s, German physicist Karl Werner Heisenberg recognized that at subatomic levels it is impossible to determine with absolute accuracy the position and momentum of moving particles; absolute certainties suddenly become relative probabilities, and most astonishing of all, it was realized that when scientists tried to observe the quantum world, they affected what was being observed.

Physicist J.S. Bell showed that if you separate two particles that have been joined, and then examine one, this act of measurement not only changes the spin of the local particle but forces the far-away particle to change in unison; one affects the other, regardless of the distance between them.

These discoveries have prompted far more than just a philosophical discussion about how atoms behave in space; they have created a debate about how subatomic processes in the human brain are connected to our conscious thoughts. This debate has undermined the traditional picture of reality by raising these questions: Is the human mind separate from the brain? If one particle can affect another across space, are we all interconnected at a fundamental level? If the human observer affects what is being observed, are we active participants in the formation of events? In quantum theory, the molecular world becomes alive with possibilities, rather than weakened by certainties. But the pivotal question is how does a possibility become an actuality? Finally, is consciousness a force in the cause-and-effect chain reaction of life?

Henry Stapp at Lawrence Berkeley Laboratory and Amit Goswami at the University of Oregon are two prominent physicists who have concluded through their own research that conscious experience is an important part of quantum reality. They even propose that consciousness is primary rather than a by-product of matter.

Nobel Laureate Brian Josephson of Cambridge University, England, is another physicist who is also willing to consider that consciousness comes first. "I am interested," he says, "in whether we should think of the world as being more centered around consciousness than is normally assumed by scientists."

"Once you begin to ask questions about states of consciousness," he adds, "you reach a region where thinking in spiritual terms is a possibility."

Josephson is presently collaborating with the Norwegian mathematician Nils Baas to develop powerful new descriptions of the mind through mathematical models. He hopes that these models will nudge us beyond the idea of the mind being fixed in the brain. "They would allow us to see the mind as something which can emerge in a wide range of circumstances, so we can envisage the mind in other forms. Some of these forms are delocalized and we can interact with them."

These physicists represent the vanguard. Most scientists remain entrenched in classical mechanics, but nonetheless, a new, sweeping scientific paradigm is taking shape. The intent of this chapter is not to debate the merit of any individual scientific theory but to look at the larger picture, particularly the implications of this paradigm shift.

The present dominant view of a mechanistic universe, Josephson believes, has led us to build a society largely based on materialistic values. "If you are working with the wrong social models, you will get the wrong results. Now presumably if the values you put in are more correct, you would get a higher quality society."

Goswami holds the same opinion. "If humans are just materialist machines without any purpose," he says, "we become valueless. By seeing consciousness as primary, then values become paramount because they are part of the true nature of ourselves."

These scientists are stressing that how we view ourselves directly affects how we view and construct reality. "In the classical worldview," submits Stapp, "each of us is just a mechanical robot, so to speak. The consequence has been a decline and almost disappearance of moral philosophy. How can you make a moral philosophy if we are all robots?"

Yet when human consciousness is seen as a driving force, then our entire self-image is profoundly altered. A new scientific image of ourselves, Stapp anticipates, "may provide the foundation of a moral order better suited to our times, a self-image that endows human life with meaning, responsibility, and a deeper linkage to nature as a whole."

TO SEE THE LIGHT

Einstein said, "Science without religion is lame; religion without science is blind." Einstein would be fascinated to learn what the new scientific story of the cosmos is teaching us about spirituality.

God said, "Let there be light," and there was light. To astrophysicist Bernhard Haisch, these words from the book of Genesis have added meaning. He and two other scientists have developed a theory that suggests light mediates the existence of the world of matter. "If this is the case," says Haisch, "it would lend support to the metaphysical concept that light is fundamental."

Haisch is a research scientist and a principle investigator on NASA projects. He is also a scientific editor of an astrophysical journal and editor-in-chief of the *Journal of Scientific Exploration*, a professional publication that scrutinizes topics outside the established disciplines of science. During the last few years, Haisch has been working with Alfonso Rueda of California State University and Harold Puthoff of the Institute for Advanced Studies in Texas, on a rigorous scientific theory that could significantly revise our understanding of how the physical universe is constructed. This research team believes that a form of light known in modern physics as the zero-point field (ZPF) may help determine the properties of matter. Moreover, it is their opinion that matter may be a secondary phenomenon.

Simply stated, ZPF is a sea of electromagnetic radiation that fills the universe. These scientists postulate that it is an intrinsic part of the universe, not just an energy forced into existence by quantum laws. They also reason that when the all-pervasive ZPF interacts with massless electric charges, it then creates the appearance of mass. In other words, mass, inertia, and gravity are all derived from this form of universal light.

"If ZPF is as real as it appears to be," says Haisch, "then it provides a potential source of energy that dwarfs anything we have discovered so far."

Haisch, though, isn't just interested in the technological implications of these findings. He once studied for the priesthood and has had a long-time interest in closing the gap between scientific and spiritual perspectives. "When you look within the esoteric literature, you constantly run across references to light," he says. "If light really is the creator of these physical properties of inertia and gravitation, then the deeper implication is that light somehow is the mediator between the nonphysical realm — which you could call the spiritual realm — and the world of matter."

To the physicist, notes Haisch, light is defined as merely electromagnetic waves or quantum photons, but to the mystic, or to people who have undergone near-death experiences, light and love seem to be intertwined as the very manifestation of the divine. Perhaps, he speculates, one is the mere projection of the other. Perhaps light is even the medium that consciousness uses to create reality. What excites Haisch is the theoretical possibility of learning more about how the physical universe acquires its most fundamental properties through light, while simultaneously exploring ancient esoteric ideas.

"Is there reason," he asks, "to think that after 350 years of increasing separation there could now be a confluence of metaphysical and scientific perspectives at the most fundamental level?"

WORKING TOGETHER

If you look at recent changes in both religious and scientific circles, it is evident that people are finding ways to cross disciplines and work together in ways that have not happened before.

In a 1992 article that physicist Brian Josephson coauthored with biophysicist Beverly Rubik, the two stressed how science is not an isolated system. It cannot be divorced from philosophy. It cannot be divorced from moral questions. "The world has suffered from the conventional fragmentary approach, its integrity violated by considering only the parts and thus losing sight of the whole," they stated.

"The new science," they advised, "as science with consciousness and conscience, will concern itself with the consequences of science to the individual, society, and the whole world: it is a science for the integrity of both people and planet that should be translatable into action."

Action invites the general public to become involved, not simply religious leaders or scientific experts. Norman Lear, the television producer, writer, director, and founder of People for the American Way, calls himself one of the "gropers" — meaning he, too, is groping for answers, especially spiritually. "We must not allow this territory to be preempted by 'experts' who claim that their distinctive theology, tradition, or sizable membership gives them a special stamp of superiority, a greater right to be heard," challenges Lear. "It is precisely this spiritual arrogance and intolerance — particularly toward us, the unaffiliated 'gropers' — that has stifled a frank, 360-degree discussion of what it means to have a living faith in this troubled time."

Lear is convinced that a growing spiritual movement composed of individuals "thirsting for spiritual unity without uniformity" is one the most striking events of this age: "It is a buzzing, disconnected eruption of spiritual reaction to our times, operating without the sanction of the popular culture or organized religion."

Lear is also convinced that spirituality is gaining a broader base because the term is more inclusive. It used to be that if you were "spiritual" you followed a certain religion, and your spirituality supposedly originated from that religion. However, says Lear, people are realizing that spirituality does not naturally or automatically flow from an outside source; spirituality is an innate human capacity. "It is not a chicken or egg situation. First, there is the original gift of the capacity. That capacity takes somebody to Hinduism, somebody to Buddhism, somebody to Christianity. We can marvel at how many different directions we can find from the same capacity, but we know that what makes us human together is the capacity."

The trouble is, he continues, we tend to overlook the fact that we all share this same starting point. "If only we could recognize the capacity the way we recognize the human nose, eyes, and ears, it might be so much easier to embrace. If only it were visible when you saw another human being."

MOVEMENT OF THE SPIRIT

Reverend Larry Thomas resides over the Community United Methodist Church in the coastal town of Half Moon Bay, California. Even in this small town he sees people's attitudes toward religious leaders changing dramatically. "One of the fundamental shifts," says Thomas, "is from an external authority to a person's internal spiritual authority. It is the authority of one's own inner journey and in many ways this is a much more demanding spirituality than the dogmatic external one. This spirituality expects individuals to do the work for themselves and not simply let the established religious authorities carry that out for them."

Thomas has also noticed that his congregation seeks spiritual confirmation from different sources, and many find inspiration in the new scientific findings that reveal the interrelatedness of all life. The contemporary scientific story of the cosmos, Thomas believes, is more mystical and much more pregnant with religious possibilities than the old reductionistic, mechanistic worldview. "There is an urgent need for us to see the world whole," he says. "We live in a historical moment when for the first time in several hundred years it is possible to be deeply religious and deeply scientific without contradiction."

We're in the middle of an extraordinary spiritual movement. While conducting research for this book, I interviewed the now-retired Archbishop Desmond Tutu, who received the 1984 Nobel Peace Prize. As the first black Anglican bishop of Johannesburg, South Africa, he devoted his life to fighting racial and political injustice. "Spirituality is not something nebulous," insists

Archbishop Tutu. "It is something that *does* change the world."

He talks about the historic changes within the last few years that have germinated from the actions of dedicated individuals and the longing of many for a world of justice and wholeness. "I feel very strongly that people deep down recognize goodness," he says. "They know we are made for something better than the status quo. You don't have to teach people that they are made for freedom and not 'unfreedom.' The breaking out of democracy and freedom in so many places has made me say that there is something called the fullness of time. Why did it happen that the Berlin Wall collapsed, or the collapse of Communism, or the adoption of democracy in South Africa and so forth? We are the beneficiaries of the prayers and the courage of what people have done in the past. Things have come to a head *now*."

He then added a comment that might seem trivial if it didn't encapsulate an entire world change: "And so there is this movement of the spirit."

CHAPTER TWO

The Caring Connection

The freight train was traveling at forty miles per hour when the engineer and the conductor spotted two small children playing on the track. Immediately the engineer pulled the emergency brake, but both he and the conductor knew the train would not stop in time. The reaction of the conductor, Anthony Falzo, was automatic. He later said, "If I had taken the time to think it would have been all over."

Falzo jumped from the train and landed on the tracks about ten feet away from the children. He took two large strides and quickly grabbed the three-year-old boy and his eighteen-month-old brother. Within the seconds left, all Falzo could do was pull the children to the ground between the tracks, using his body to cover theirs. They were all found lying under the third car of the nineteen-car train when it finally stopped.

The youngest boy had been struck in the face by the locomotive's plow just before Falzo pulled him to the ground, but otherwise the two children, who had wandered from their nearby home onto the unfenced tracks, were not seriously injured. Falzo wasn't hurt either, although the clearance between the train and his body was so tight that the back of his insulated vest was slashed.

This train conductor risked his own life to save the lives of the children, but his heroism is not uncommon. On the other hand, many turn their backs on those in trouble.

Would Anthony Falzo have risked his life to save a grown man or woman, instead of two children on the train tracks? He probably would have still tried to help, but Falzo admits that some of his colleagues are openly callous toward adults who, in their rush to get somewhere, ignore warning signals and calculatedly drive across tracks, trying to beat approaching trains. "I've heard conductors and engineers say, 'If this guy wants to be a jerk and he gets hit, that's his problem,'" he says.

Upon investigating what encourages or discourages acts of heroism or altruism, or what prompts compassion and empathy, we enter a maze of contradictions. Essentially, all relationships between families and friends flourish or falter depending upon how much we care for one another; our very survival as a species hinges upon the ability to love, nurture, and protect our young. Nevertheless, over the centuries we have erected psychological and physical walls between tribes, villages, neighborhoods, races, and nations. Human actions are dictated by boundaries between those for whom we feel responsible and those we don't, for those to whom we feel an emotional commitment, and those we avoid or specifically oppose.

DISCOVERING EMPATHY

Psychologist Martin Hoffman observed in his studies on empathy that if people view victims as responsible for their own plight, or conclude that their fate is deserved, the response to the victim may be indifference or even contempt.

Thus people often ignore people begging for money on the streets, justifying their apathy by convincing themselves that the homeless somehow caused or deserved their problems. Moreover, although we agree it is immoral to settle a conflict between individuals through murder, the world's leaders see nothing wrong with ordering armies to kill one another to settle conflicts between countries.

Heartlessness, double standards, and the willingness to wage war have led many behavioral scientists to conclude that the human being's capacity to care for others is driven by self-interest. As for those who rescue people from burning buildings — or train tracks — psychologists have also been suspicious of their heroism, arguing that perhaps they feared feeling guilty or ashamed if they hadn't saved the victims, or conversely, perhaps they anticipated an emotional reward for their bravery.

Psychologist Daniel Batson says that for years it was assumed all humans were basically self-serving. Empathy, altruism, and acting for the public good were not even considered worthy of further scientific inquiry. "The question of whether we care for others or only for ourselves is one of the few to which psychologists of all stripes, researchers and practitioners, implicitly give a common answer," he writes. "Psychology's implicit answer is that the only persons we are capable of caring about, ultimately, are ourselves. We value others instrumentally; we care for their welfare only to the degree that it affects ours."

This cynical view of ourselves, however, is now being challenged. During the last decade, Batson and other social psychologists have conducted a series of experiments expressly designed to test whether the motive for helping others stems from altruism or moral principles, or whether humans are simply social egoists, offering help only when it benefits them in some way. According to Batson, these experiments indicate the human ability to care unselfishly for others is far greater than believed.

At the same time, Batson is also acutely aware that many of us still try to avoid the full expression of empathy. "Lest we feel too much, we turn the corner, switch channels, flip the page, or think of something else," he writes.

Signs of avoidance might be confirmation of human limitations, but Batson asks a thought-provoking question: "Could this apparent necessity to defend ourselves against feeling empathy be a clue to the magnitude of our capacity to care?"

We will probably never know the extent of our caring capacity, he says, until we overcome our present cultural barriers to nurturing what he calls "the fragile flower of altruistic caring." He cautions: "Before we can do this, however, we need to know the flower is there. Psychology, including social psychology, has assumed that it is not."

THE HEART OF THE MIND

As scientists reexamine these assumptions, they have found that empathy even appears to be a key player in the evolution of the human brain. Paul MacLean, senior research scientist at the Clinical Brain Disorders Branch of the National Institute of Mental Health Neuroscience Center, points out that our brain has evolved into a hierarchy of three brains in one — a triune brain — with the two oldest brain formations reflecting our ancestral ties to reptiles and early mammals.

Appearing late in evolution is the neomammalian brain, with its elaborate neocortex. The neocortex operates somewhat like a heartless computer. If this part of the brain had been left unbridled in humans, says MacLean, we might all have become Frankensteins without consciences. Yet during the evolutionary process from Neanderthal to Cro-Magnon, a new formation in the brain developed that allows us to gain insight into other people's feelings. Specifically, a prefrontal cortex evolved underneath a heightened brow; it is this prefrontal cortex that distinguishes us as subjective individuals, allowing us to receive knowledge not only from the external world, but also from our private internal world.

"The prefrontal cortex is the only neocortex that looks inward to the inside world," reports MacLean. "Clinically, there is evidence that the prefrontal cortex, by looking inward, so to speak, obtains the gut feelings required for identifying with another individual. It is this new development that makes possible the insight required for the foresight to plan for the needs of others as well as the self — to use our knowledge to alleviate suffering everywhere."

MacLean, like Batson, poses a philosophical question. "Why, slowly but progressively," he asks, "did nature add something to the neocortex that for the first time brings a heart and a sense of compassion into the world? Altruism, empathy — these are almost new words."

A WHOLE NEW VIEW OF THE HEART

The medical profession used to view the heart as simply a pump that kept blood circulating through the body, but in today's world, doctors appear to be agreeing with mystics and artists who have always pictured the heart as the center of the personality. Science is proving what throughout the ages we have instinctively suspected: love, compassion, and other positive emotions really do radiate power — the power to affect us mentally, as well as physically.

Several years ago, Dr. Redford Williams, a professor at Duke University Medical Center, demonstrated that people who frequently express anger, hostility, and cynicism were far more prone to heart attacks. At that time he outlined the steps people could take to reduce these toxic responses to life. As he said, "trusting hearts last longer."

Today, we have gained more knowledge about the benefits of loving states. Dr. Andrew Armour, a researcher at the department of physiology and biophysics at Dalhousie University, Nova Scotia, has identified an intrinsic nervous system within the heart that is far more extensive and crucial to our health than ever imagined. When Armour explains how the heart operates, he describes it as having its own small brain. "We have mapped afferents, which receive input, and efferents, which put out information, and thousands of neurons connecting these two," he says. "This 'computer' is hard-wired to all parts of your body. Therefore, if you scratch your knee because there is an itch, the neurons in your heart will have that information. When you get up to run, the heart already anticipates this action."

As a physician treating heart disease, Armour hopes these findings will empower patients. People, he says, are more likely to modify harmful behavior if they realize the heart is not just a pump or piece of plumbing but rather a self-corrective, intelligent organ.

How is this information related to caring and compassion? The Institute of HeartMath, a nonprofit organization based in California, is presently conducting pioneering research on how the heart literally influences our thoughts and actions. One of their goals is to "scientifically and mathematically prove the correlation between spirit and matter."

Rollin McCraty, director of research for HeartMath, explains that the heart is an electrical power center, producing electrical amplitude approximately fifty times more powerful than the brain's; these electrical signals permeate every cell in the body. With the aid of modern computers, the researchers at HeartMath have accurately measured beat-to-beat variations in heart rate, and determined that emotional reactions in the brain are linked to electrical changes in the heart and nervous system, which in turn produce hormonal and immune-system changes. It is an intricate mind-brain-heart communication system.

For instance, a negative emotion like frustration changes the heart rhythm to a random, jerky pattern, while feelings of compassion or sincere appreciation result in a harmonious heart rhythm. The smooth, harmonious pattern indicates that the two nervous systems — the sympathetic and parasympathetic pathways — are exquisitely synchronized. A balance between these two systems increases cardiovascular efficiency, and influences hormonal and immune-system responses. In one study, when individuals focused on compassion while listening to music designed to elicit positive emotions, their levels of the antibody secretory IgA increased; IgA is an integral part of the body's immune system.

This is proof that positive and negative emotions affect our physiology quite differently. Positive states are clearly healthier. However, the researchers are finding that the heart affects not just the body but also the brain. The chain reaction they are detecting involves a two-way sensory system. The electrical patterns of the heart are relayed back to the brain and our higher brain centers respond in dramatically different ways to these patterns. When the heart rhythms are jerky due to anxiety or anger, the cortex becomes inhibited, clouding our thinking and slowing our reactions. Smooth, harmonious heart rhythms have the opposite effect on the brain; our perceptions are clearer, our creativity greater. To a certain extent, the human mind is orchestrated by these rhythms of the heart.

"What is really fascinating," McCraty says, "is how the heart is directly affecting brain function and our perception of reality. And this is measurable."

Can we change our reality so it is colored more by love and caring than anger and cynicism? Researchers believe we can, and it is these next steps that hold so much hope for humanity. At Heart-Math they are using a technique called "Freeze Frame," which teaches people how to stop negative reactive emotions. "The advantage of this technique," stresses McCraty, "is that it works in the moment. You can even apply the technique while talking to a person on the telephone."

People can undergo comprehensive training to learn the "Freeze Frame" technique, but, simply stated, the process starts with recognizing stressful feelings as soon as they arise. "Immediately, when you sense the stress," McCraty says, "you need to shift your attention to the area of your heart. We suggest you imagine breathing right through the center of your heart and chest. The next step is to change your emotional state to a positive one."

It helps for people to recall pleasant times in their life or focus on a feeling of appreciation, such as appreciating the fact they have a home or a job. Yet it is at this stage that some people get stuck, continues McCraty, because they try to *think* about positive emotions instead of *feeling* them. This difference is the key, because the technique's purpose is to cause changes — through feelings — to the physiology. After testing individuals in their laboratory, says McCraty, they have found that when people maintain a positive frame of mind, then their heart, head, and brain waves are all brought into optimal synchronization. "When that happens, really profound perceptual shifts occur. Everybody who has experienced this process reports a whole new level of intuitive ability. They are able to draw on answers they didn't have previously. They seem to bring in more of the heart wisdom to the linear, logical mind."

People have always tried to teach love and the finer human qualities, but today these higher ideals are becoming easier and easier to access. In no other age have we had so many opportunities for self-development. A wide variety of methods and workshops are available to help individuals reduce stress, heal addictions, resolve inner and outer conflict, and generally enhance living.

The motivation for change is often driven by pragmatic concerns. The HeartMath Institute, for example, has been holding training sessions with corporations reeling from absenteeism, poor performance, and growing health costs — all related in some way to stress. But the value of self-help workshops and therapeutic sessions stretches far beyond job or health benefits. As individuals venture into self-exploration, they often begin to think differently, as well as act differently, toward the external forces governing their existence.

All the same, self-development in adults is a catch-up process. The place to begin cultivating the best human qualities and teaching the art of caring is with children.

DEVELOPING EMPATHY IN CHILDREN

Most experts agree that, to a great extent, empathy is learned — preferably through example at a young age. "We must," writes Paul MacLean, "consider the possibility that if it is not taught and learned during a critically receptive period in the brain's development, it may never be fully awakened."

When Carolyn Zahn-Waxler and Marian Radke-Yarrow at the National Institute of Mental Health conducted a series of studies on the development of empathy and altruism in children, they found that children as young as two years of age can interpret, in simple ways, the physical and psychological states of others. Yet they also documented that the capacity of young children to reach out to others in need is shaped by their socialization. Abused children are not only more aggressive toward their friends but have difficulty responding to a peer's distress, whereas children who are securely attached to caregivers empathize with others far more easily.

Children raised in a stable home, however, do not automatically develop compassion. The capacity to care seems to be greatly influenced by how a youngster is taught to handle distress. For instance, when psychologists Mark Barnett and Sandra McCoy studied children who had endured distressful events, such as a serious illness in the family, they found that empathy mainly developed in the youngsters who were encouraged to experience their emotions during difficult times. By expressing their own feelings these children learned how to respond to others.

Unfortunately, many children grow up in households where they are not allowed to express anger or sorrow. Ervin Staub, a psychologist at the University of Massachusetts, calls attention to the fact that before the twentieth century, children were viewed as innately willful. The goal was to rear obedient children, but to obtain such obedience, a child's will was often intentionally broken by rigid emotional constraints or physical punishment.

These parental practices are changing, but Staub maintains that we need far more education about how certain methods of raising children can erase empathy and lead to aggression in adults. "When you tell people that children should receive love and good care," Staub says, "and that parents should respond to the needs of children, most people, at least in principle, would respond, 'Of course!' But the circumstances of life for many families nowadays are such that parents do not have the peace of mind or the structure in their lives to provide these conditions for their children. In order to be caring and loving to children, to be sensitive to their needs, to have the patience that children require, it is necessary to lead a reasonably ordered life, and for adults to have their basic needs met."

When unemployment increases, so does child abuse. When economic problems accelerate, so does societal violence. We must pursue, entreats Staub, social legislation and social mores that support families, so that their basic financial, physical, and emotional needs are met. Although there is no guarantee that families will then, in turn, provide the kind of foundation for their children that induces caring relationships, he argues that the stakes are so high, we at least have to make a serious effort in this direction.

"I am suggesting that changes are required not only for humanitarian reasons," says Staub, "not only to improve the quality of life for many and create greater social justice, but also to contribute to positive socialization on a societal scale, which is essential for the evolution of human connection, caring, and nonaggression."

A MATTER OF PRIORITIES

All politicians, whether conservative or liberal, say they want to help children, but child neglect, and the proportion of children living in extreme poverty, continues to grow at an alarming rate. Ultimately, how one chooses to address societal inequities becomes an independent moral judgment.

Psychologist Martin Hoffman, who has examined the links between empathy, moral judgment, and justice, presents these two approaches to inequity: "Suppose one is deciding the fairest way to distribute society's resources. If one empathizes with society's least advantaged people and imagines the consequences of different distributive systems for them, one may advocate distributive systems based on the principle of need, or equality. If one empathizes with people who work hard and save for their families, one might advocate a distributive system based on effort."

Such decisions sound cut and dried, but consider the following hypothetical game devised by John Rawls, a James Bryant Conant University Emeritus Professor at Harvard University. His book *A Theory of Justice* is considered a classic on the subject of ethics and justice. In the game that Rawls designed, the participants are given an opportunity to construct an "ideal" society. They are offered choices to ensure basic liberties and economic security, but the game has two inhibiting rules: The participants have to make these choices without knowing their own race, gender, religion, social status, or class position — the "veil of ignorance" constraint. The second rule simply states that once the players make their decision on how to distribute the resources of a society, they cannot change their minds, even if they discover their decisions do not serve their own self-interests.

Rawls theorized that because participants couldn't guarantee their position in society, and might end up as one of its least advantaged members, they would be inclined to construct a just society, one that distributed goods and services to maximize benefits for everyone. While Rawls's hypothesis has never been tested scientifically, it is so provocative that it continues to be widely discussed and debated.

Rawls is advocating a balanced mix of merit-based and need-based justice — capitalism steered by social conscience. He recommends rewarding people according to their contributions to society, or the excellence of a product, as long as goods and services are not pursued at the expense of the least advantaged, and not distributed in a manner that results in drastic inequalities.

What intrigues psychologist Martin Hoffman about Rawls's theory of justice is not what might happen in a game, but what could happen in *real life*. In the game, the motivation for constructing a just society stems from the players' fear that they might be allotted a position of poverty in life. What shapes decisions in real life, asks Hoffman, when fear is taken away? How are political and personal choices made when a person is financially secure due to talent, hard work, or hereditary advantages, and you ask that individual to accept a system that helps the least advantaged, and possibly requires some compromise?

"The answer," writes Hoffman, "must include a motive to help others that is powerful enough at least to operate as a constraint on the individual's self-interest. Rawls's theory lacks such a motive, but there is one available — empathy."

COMPASSION IN ACTION

The enormous difference one person can make in this world by operating from a pure motive to help others often takes us by surprise. Inspiring examples exist to demonstrate how relatively simple it is to move beyond just wishing for a better world to actually doing something about it. Such an example is Muhammad Yunus, who founded the Grameen Bank in Bangladesh over twenty years ago to help the poorest of the poor. The Grameen Bank model has spread from a small project in one Bangladesh village to a global movement; his innovative microcredit program now has the potential to drastically decrease poverty worldwide.

In 1976, Muhammad Yunus, an economics professor, was distressed to see the suffering caused in his country by a nationwide famine. He decided to loan a little money from his own pocket (the equivalent of a couple of dollars) to several people. That small amount of money not only allowed these few people to fend off starvation, but helped them regain pride and buy materials so they could work. Yunus then established a nationwide bank in Bangladesh, based on the same principle of making small loans of less than $50 to poor people who had no assets for collateral. This is also a story about placing trust in a person's honesty; the Grameen Bank has a near-perfect repayment rate.

Today, the Grameen Bank lends more than $500 million a year to 2 million borrowers, and microcredit projects exist in over fifty countries, including the United States. The Grameen Bank continues to experience almost no defaults on these loans. It is estimated that this microcredit movement has helped over 36 million people worldwide, and the goal is to reach 100 million of the world's poorest families by 2005.

Ninety-four percent of the bank's borrowers in Bangladesh are women. "When we help women," says Yunus, "we help their children, so you are contributing to the next generation. It's not just simply overcoming a problem of the day. You are building a new future, completely."

Yunus adamantly asserts that the poor do not create poverty. "People say the poor are poor because they are lazy, don't have skills, or don't have initiative. That is wrong. The real problem is not the poor. The real problem is the institutions that deny them the opportunity they deserve."

Yunus has been to the White House to discuss his ideas, but although President Clinton and other politicians support the microcredit concept, Yunus knows it is hard to get governments and institutions to dramatically change policies, especially policies regarding money and poverty. For the most part, innovative changes, stirred by compassion for the less fortunate, are occurring because of private citizens.

INVESTING IN WOMEN TO ENRICH THE WORLD

One of the most promising developments is the growth of nongovernmental groups that are improving the human condition on a global level. Anne Firth Murray is the founder of The Global Fund for Women, a nonprofit organization engaged in investing time and money in women's causes. While some consider the women's movement yesterday's issue in the Western world, women continue to struggle against inequality and oppression.

"As we change the relationships between men and women," says Murray, "we are changing the very nature of each society. We are moving from societies based on difference, of one group being over another — whether it is educated/uneducated, male/female, white/black — to a world where people can interact in a more equal way. If we can get to the point where across the great divide of sex we can treat each other with respect, love, and compassion, then we may be able to do it in other areas. The global women's movement is the most hopeful and inclusive movement in the world today."

The Global Fund for Women assists groups with grants averaging just over $6,000, to a maximum of $10,000. This money has made the difference between surviving and thriving to a group in Papua, New Guinea, that is helping women and girls in rural villages read and write effectively in their own language, and to an organization in Turkey dedicated to supplying women at the grassroots level with tools and strategies to confront inequality. Since 1987, this organization has given more than $6 million to over 700 women's groups around the world.

"The way we do philanthropy is different from the way philanthropy has been done in the past," says Murray, explaining that they encourage women to devise their own plan to solve specific problems. "We give money, but we ask them what they think is the best thing to do for women and for society. They have the plan, vision, and commitment, and we provide the venture capital, and require accountability. It becomes a contractual relationship to get a job done."

By encouraging women in each country to initiate their own programs, and by forming a network linking women's groups worldwide, the Global Fund for Women is spreading — in addition to money — a powerful message that when you care enough to lend a helping hand, society is the beneficiary, not just individuals.

A WHOLE NEW APPROACH TO VIOLENCE

Eliciting compassion when discussing poverty is relatively easy, but attitudes surrounding violence are much less forgiving. Although compassion exists for victims, the general public has shown little concern about how to prevent creating criminals in the first place. Like other aspects of society, violence has been compartmentalized; our response and responsibility is parceled out to the criminal justice system, which determines blame and punishment. Consequently, we have become very good at arresting people, but have done a poor job of arresting violence itself.

Even the medical profession has become used to reacting to violence with detachment, only treating the results. Dr. Deborah Prothrow-Stith is assistant dean and professor of public health practice at the Harvard School of Public Health. As a medical student working in an emergency room, she treated a young man who had been stabbed. As she stitched his slashed body, he admitted that he had been in a fight and he planned to seek revenge as soon as he got out of the hospital.

Prothrow-Stith was shocked — not that the man had been stabbed; she was used to seeing the scars of violence. What disturbed her the most was that although this man fully intended to fight again, the hospital policy was not to intervene. If he had threatened suicide she could have ordered a psychiatric evaluation, but at that time, in the late '70s, there was no standard medical procedure to calm anger and prevent further violence. Patients were stitched up and sent back into their private wars without any counseling.

Yet, thanks to Prothrow-Stith and others who contend that violence is not inevitable, the subject of prevention is now being taken more seriously. "Once in a while there is just a breakthrough in the way we think about problems and this is one," she states.

The breakthrough is the recognition that violence is a public health issue, that a parallel exists between preventing violence and preventing disease. For instance, once we acknowledged that cigarettes kill people, groups formed to encourage individuals never to start smoking. Other groups help people quit. The battle against cigarette addiction isn't over, but our society is now equipped with many preventive strategies. The same multifaceted public health approach, Prothrow-Stith reasons, has to be taken with violence.

Prothrow-Stith's approach to violence is laced with compassion, but she knows that calling for a strong national public policy to counteract violence is one of the hardest areas to inject the heart and human spirit. "People argue that interventive techniques are a bleeding heart way of dealing with the problem," she says, "but what I say is that if we want to prevent lung cancer we couldn't do it with just lung surgery. We're not going to prevent violence with more arrests and incarceration. So for me, it is not a liberal, conservative, or progressive ideology. It just makes sense."

A recent study by the Justice Department's Bureau of Justice Statistics revealed that more than one-third of inmates were unemployed before they were arrested, and almost half had an income of less than $600 a month; 48 percent of female inmates and 13 percent of males had been physically or sexually abused in their lives; 60 percent used drugs or alcohol at the time of their offense; and almost one-third had parents or guardians who misused alcohol and drugs.

To counter these problems, Prothrow-Stith has created The Community Violence Prevention Project through the Harvard School of Public Health. They have accumulated information about a wide variety of programs that have proven effective, such as gang-prevention initiatives, parenting workshops, dating violence prevention courses, and adolescent job and life skills training. Because the options vary so much, they offer an intervention program with a how-to guide, so citizens can tailor the programs to meet the needs of each community. Prothrow-Stith has also developed a Violence Prevention Curriculum for Adolescents, which has been used by thousands of schools in the United States, as well as other countries.

VOLUNTEERING FROM THE HEART

Another direct way to underscore our common humanity and serve others who need help the most is to volunteer. Empathy can readily be expressed in words, but when it translates into voluntary work, then it creates forever-binding connections between people. Volunteering has a long history, but only within the last few years have schools taken volunteering more seriously.

In Maryland, for example, the State Board of Education approved a plan requiring all public school students to become involved in community service in order to graduate from high school.

What makes the Maryland program different is that it is built into the curriculum so that students first study a social problem (such as homelessness) before they take any action. Afterward, the students debate the effectiveness of their actions and what else they could do to help the problem. The challenge is to deliver more than just scraps of charity — to help others in a way that contributes to their dignity and independence.

Maryland's community service program is called a "service-learning process" — study it, do it, and reflect upon it — and this process is being copied by other states. Many colleges are also urging a formal commitment to service as part of one's education in life.

For more than two decades, the Independent Sector, a national coalition of over 800 organizations involved with philanthropy and volunteerism, has been tracking who gives, why they serve others, and how to boost volunteerism. "Most of the people who volunteer as adults have volunteered as children," says Virginia Hodgkinson, a senior consultant for Independent Sector, and research professor at Georgetown Public Policy Institute at Georgetown University. "We have found that the younger you are when you get exposed to volunteering, the more likely you are to maintain that habit through life."

Hodgkinson maintains that we have to cultivate the capacity to care in children and then teach them how to act upon that instinct. "At a time when civil society is in question," she says, "at a time when people feel they are losing control of the economy and the government, volunteering offers individuals a way to solve common problems. Volunteering holds this fragile democracy together."

At present, nearly 93 million volunteers are actively participating in a variety of causes throughout the United States. The following story demonstrates what is possible when people care enough to offer their time and talent to serve others.

Since the 1980s, Henry Gaskins and his wife Mary Ann have been running Freedom Youth Academy, a nonprofit volunteer organization that provides free after-school academic guidance to kids. Students from all parts of Washington, D.C., arrive at the Gaskins' home late in the afternoon. Many of these students have been marked as "failures" by their teachers, and their own parents are often high school dropouts who cannot help them academically or single parents who are too busy grappling with their own survival.

Mary Ann tutors the children from kindergarten to the 7th grade, while Henry, who holds a Ph.D. in adult education, tutors the older students, specifically preparing them for college entrance exams. Within months, the majority of their students exceed the average SAT scores for both whites and minorities, and many have gone on to the nation's top colleges.

Henry and Mary Ann Gaskins have five children of their own, who have also attended top universities on scholarships. When asked why they have been so successful with not only their own children but also with the students who arrive at their home seeking help, they answer that it is partly because they offer each student individualized attention. Equally important, their loving home environment supplies much-needed affection, thereby developing students' self-esteem.

"We've been blessed," Henry Gaskins says. "We have raised five children, and we have been able to hold down full-time jobs and remain healthy, and we just feel that with these blessings we had to give something back to the community."

In one speech at a PTA meeting, Henry Gaskins also talked about how we all have the responsibility to help the children in our community if we want to stop high drop-out rates and prevent illiteracy: "The community must become the extended family it once was and provide the role models and support to guide and sustain those in the next generation. Our future as a people depends on it. Our love for humanity demands it!"

ALTRUISM AND WHOLENESS

People usually equate altruism with self-sacrifice, but many who willingly serve others say their actions are not based on self-denial. On the contrary, they emphasize that volunteering brings them self-fulfillment. For instance, under no circumstances do Rod and Patti Radle regard themselves as martyrs, although by outward appearances they look as if they have denied themselves many basic material comforts in life. The Radles have not only devoted their lives to helping the poor, but they have also chosen to live among the poor in San Antonio.

Since 1972, this couple has served as codirectors of Inner City Development, an all-volunteer agency in San Antonio that supplies emergency and support services for poverty-stricken families, who are mostly Mexican Americans. The Radles are dedicated

Christians who made a decision before they married to live their lives "not just *talking* about doing worthwhile things, but doing it."

Because the Radles are not paid for their work at Inner City Development, they take turns holding formal jobs that can bring in a paycheck to support themselves and their children. They have never chased material wealth. When they were invited to the White House to receive an award for their volunteer work, Rod borrowed a tie and Patti borrowed a dress.

They say material goods mean little to them. What means the most? "Number one is human contact," answers Patti Radle. "It's the intangible things, such as our relationships with people."

Patti elaborates by describing an incident that occurred when she and Rod first moved into the neighborhood. "A girl with no shoes asked Rod to pop the infected blisters on her feet," she says. "Then she gave me a pin broach. I knew this girl didn't have much, and yet she was giving this pin to me. It was so touching, and the pin has always reminded me that it caused her greater joy to have something to give to me than to have that pin herself. What she got out of it was pleasing me, and I think this is what happens to us when we do things for others."

When psychologists Anne Colby and William Damon studied the lives of individuals who demonstrate an extraordinary moral commitment to society, they found that their moral convictions were indistinguishable from their personal conduct. "We saw," says Damon, "very little, if any, discrepancy between their perceptions of who they are, and their perceptions of what they believe they ought to do in a moral sense."

Colby and Damon recognize that this type of internal and external unity between self, morality, and social action is not common. Moral beliefs often come in conflict with one's career or family obligations. "Most people," explains Damon, "will say, 'I give to charity, and I care about these people, but I can only give so much, or I can only do so much.'"

In contrast, the subjects of their study did not separate their moral ideals from personal and professional goals. How they conducted their lives, the work they did, and their interpersonal relationships were all woven into the moral choices they made. "There was," says Damon, "very little compartmentalization between self-understanding, moral belief, and social engagement."

This research substantiates that it is possible to translate our ideals into action. Although these moral exemplars are exceptional people, their extraordinary acts of compassion and generosity confirm virtues that are rooted within us all.

The Dalai Lama, the spiritual and political leader of the Tibetan people, once said, "Helping other people, concern for other people is now a matter of global survival. In practical reality, concern for other people is finally how you get the best result. On the contrary, if we are negligent and ignorantly degrade other people, if we think just of our own home, our own small environment, and we are negligent to others, eventually we will all lose. We will all have to face these consequences."

It may be naive to think that empathy or compassion alone can change the world. It may be naive to think that exceptional acts of unselfish love or the work of dedicated volunteers alone can make a difference on a large scale. Obviously a massive reshuffling of political priorities is required, and a dramatic change in the way we conduct business and educate children. But if these changes are based on compassion and empathy for others, there is a chance we can create a better world. That's not naive. As the next chapters show, we are learning it is possible.

CHAPTER THREE

Healing Ourselves to Heal Society

Every country and every century has had its anecdotes about individuals beating a doctor's fatal prognosis through prayer, a fierce will to live, or some other inexplicable victory of mind over matter. These stories have finally been put to the test in the laboratory, and modern research has demonstrated that the mind does indeed influence the healing process. We are also realizing that for the healing process to be complete, the entire spectrum of consciousness needs to be involved, including the human spirit.

Slowly but firmly, whole-person medicine is reforming our present mechanistic medical system, which treats the parts of the body separately, as if they are pieces of a machine that need to be repaired. Numerous writings by such well-known healers as Andrew Weil, Larry Dossey, Deepak Chopra, Jon Kabat-Zinn, Dean Ornish, and others, have already educated millions about the extensive experiments being conducted on mind-body-spirit interactions. A few of these studies will be highlighted here, but the purpose of this chapter is to move beyond the mechanics of how we heal to explore the ramifications of these healings.

Whole-person medicine is a revolutionary concept because it is changing not just how we view health but how we live. The systemic approach teaches us to look at the whole picture, all facets of a person's life, all factors that contribute to well-being. Patients know from experience that a debilitating or life-threatening illness awakens them to what is wrong with their lives, as well as to what is wrong with their bodies. Suddenly they have neither the time nor energy to clutter day-to-day existence with unimportant things. Destructive habits, attitudes, and relationships get sorted out, and if necessary tossed out, leaving space for only what matters and has meaning. The traumatic jolt from a serious illness — or any adversity — can also increase compassion and empathy for others.

Obviously not all people are affected this way. For some, an illness or hardship results in only minor changes in the way they think and live. Even so, when the art of healing is at its best, it has the potential to bring out the best in us, and when transformations do occur, it is often the ill person who can teach the well person how to *live* well.

This chapter also stresses the connection between our own well-being and the well-being of society; actions that can either harm or benefit *us* can harm or benefit the world around us. We are discovering that the same procedures, attitudes, and loving skills that increase health in ourselves can be put to use, with collective power, to increase the health of our planet. Consequently, the personal stories and the laboratory findings that follow are relevant to all of us; we do not need to wait until we are ill to learn how to redirect our lives and activate the essence of healing.

LEARNING HOW TO LIVE

Both doctors and patients often mention how an illness changes a person's perspective on life. Rachel Naomi Remen, author of *Kitchen Table Wisdom*, is the medical director of the Commonweal Cancer Help Program in California. She is also the founder and director of the Institute for the Study of Health and Illness, a training program for physicians who treat patients with life-threatening illnesses. When speaking about healing, she draws not only on her professional knowledge as a physician but also on personal experience as a patient. Dr. Remen has Crohn's disease, a chronic condition of the intestine, and she has faced major surgery several times. At fifteen, when she first became ill, she was told she would die before turning forty. She is now over fifty.

In 1981, at the time of her sixth surgery, her physician made a comment she has never forgotten: "He put his arms around me and said, 'Rachel, you must never give up hope for healing. This is a very mysterious disease and sometimes it simply goes away for reasons that we do not understand. You must keep looking within for the handles of your own healing."

Dr. Remen has come to believe that all curing is amplified by caring and compassion. "I think doctors need to recognize that their capacity to help goes beyond the power of their technology," she says. "Our real power is not in our CAT scans or chemotherapies. These are only our tools. Our real power has to do with our ability to evoke people's own innate ability to heal. Illness changes an individual. People are always growing and an illness has a tremendous influence on that process. Suffering often enables people to come to a deep realization about themselves, their relationships, and the purpose of life."

A serious illness, she says, can even strip away the habitual layers of one's personality to expose a wiser self. "Most of us have been afraid to look within. It is as if we have feared that at our core there is something unworthy. Yet many people find, in their encounter with illness, a true greatness, which may take them by surprise. It has grown in them despite their fear, anger, and bitterness. It is possible in a time of physical vulnerability to have an accelerated emotional, intellectual, and even spiritual healing. The body may become less and yet the person may become more whole. It happens all the time."

MIND-BODY-SPIRIT COMMUNICATION

If healing accelerates a change in consciousness, it helps to understand the new discoveries about how human consciousness operates. As mentioned in chapter 2, a complex mind-body-heart communication system has been identified by the Institute of HeartMath. HeartMath's experiments, plus research by other scientists, offer radical proof that human consciousness does not emanate purely from the brain. This alters our entire perception of the healing process. For instance, scientists have discovered that information is relayed between the body and brain through various behavior-modifying chemicals, as well as the well-known neurotransmitters. A leading pioneer of this research is neuropharmacologist Candace Pert, who once made this provocative statement: "In the beginning of my work, I matter-of-factly presumed that emotions were in the head or the brain. Now I would say they are really in the body as well. They are expressed in the body and are part of the body. I can no longer make a strong distinction between the brain and the body."

Pert and her colleagues began their work by looking at how drugs alter consciousness. What aroused Pert's curiosity was that although such drugs as opium and morphine are produced outside the human body, there are receptor sites for them inside the human being. So she searched for — and found — one of the brain's own natural opiates, a chemical substance known as a neuropeptide.

Researchers have now identified other neuropeptides, many of them natural analogs of psychoactive drugs; all of them have their own receptor sites in the body. That is why when people say they have a "gut feeling" about something, they often do — because the stomach and gut are dotted with receptor sites.

Pert describes the mind-body connection as an elaborate information network. Neuropeptides act as the information carriers that "speak," while their receptor sites "listen." Happy or sad feelings do not remain in the head. They affect us right down to our individual cells. This communication network is directly linked to the immune system and so is very relevant to the healing process.

Pert even challenges the phrase "mind over matter," saying the phrase is too limiting: "I think it is possible now to conceive of mind and consciousness as an emanation of emotional information processing, and as such, mind and consciousness would appear to be independent of brain and body."

THE HEART OF HEALING

How does this information translate into beneficial ways of treating patients? Ironically, as we learn more about how emotions interact with the body, particularly the heart, the area of medicine most affected is heart disease.

In the United States, heart disease remains the leading cause of death. It is known that diet, exercise, and the elimination of smoking can reduce the risk of heart disease, but most cardiologists thought it impossible to reverse blockages in coronary arteries without cholesterol-lowering drugs or surgery. Then along came Dean Ornish with research that demonstrated how heart disease patients could reverse artery blockages by changing their lifestyle alone.

Ornish is an assistant clinical professor at the University of California, San Francisco, and president of the nonprofit Preventive Medicine Research Institute. Before explaining his research, it is important to look at what shaped Ornish's own views about health and disease. During a lengthy interview with this doctor, who has been recognized by *Life* magazine as one of the fifty most influential members of his generation, Ornish revealed that as a premed student he had a roommate who was one of the few people in the country with a perfect SAT score. In a climate of such rigorous academic competition, Ornish began to feel he was not as smart as other students. The more he worried about his own capabilities, the harder it became for him to study, which made him worry even more. He had trouble sleeping, became emotionally and physically fatigued, and in this state contracted mononucleosis.

"There is a saying," comments Ornish, "that when a student is ready, a teacher appears. That was certainly true for me." Ornish's older sister was studying yoga at that time with Swami Satchidananda, and Ornish met the Swami at his parents' home. "Swami Satchidananda gave a little talk in our living room, which was really unusual back in 1972 in Dallas, Texas," he reflects.

It was this talk that inspired Ornish to study yoga and start meditating. Slowly, his mind became calmer and his health returned. He ended up graduating first in his class and giving the commencement address. In retrospect, Ornish feels that his illness, as well as the emotional turmoil he underwent, taught him how any kind of pain can act as a powerful catalyst for transformation.

"I don't think it requires a catastrophic illness to change," he says. "I do think it requires pain to change in most cases. After all, if your life is just the way you want it to be, why change it? There's no shortage of pain or suffering in the world. The issue is getting people to be aware. That's why I believe awareness of pain is the first step in healing. The second step is the awareness that you can do something about it. The third is the awareness that it really makes a difference if you do."

From a medical viewpoint, Ornish has seen what happens when people pay little attention to how they are feeling. Using a poignant metaphor, he observes that individuals who bypass their emotions sometimes have to face bypass surgery. "Real healing," he says, "comes when you open your heart. It's a different kind of open-heart surgery, you might say. Opening the heart means that you let down those barriers that keep you isolated and keep you thinking you are separate."

It is the perception of isolation that seems to cause the most emotional pain, believes Ornish. Practically all the world's religions have tried to teach us how to replace a sense of separation with a sense of unity with all creation, but Ornish stresses that one does not have to follow any particular religion to experience being part of something larger than ourselves.

To prove that heart disease can be healed by "opening one's heart," and changing behavior patterns, Ornish designed a program for heart patients that requires them to quit smoking, exercise for an hour three times a week, and change their diet to eliminate practically all animal products. But Ornish's program does not stop at diet and exercise. His patients attend support groups and practice such mind-body techniques as yoga, meditation, and guided imagery. They learn to pay attention to not only their physical bodies but also to their emotions, reactions, and the way they live their lives.

Ornish's work has received a great deal of publicity, but most of the media have focused on his recommendations for a healthy diet. What is overlooked is that Ornish is teaching us about love. To get his point across about the healing power of intimacy, Ornish has now written a book called *Love & Survival.* He writes, "Love and intimacy are at a root of what makes us sick and what makes us well, what causes sadness and what brings happiness, what makes us suffer and what leads to healing. If a new drug had the same impact, virtually every doctor in the country would be recommending it for their patients."

THE MEDICAL-SPIRITUAL REVOLUTION

Surprisingly, the medical profession is leading the way in acknowledging the power of love and spirituality. Until recently Western doctors not only ignored the spiritual component in healing, they were extremely wary of discussing it. A few years ago, David Larson, president of the National Institute for Healthcare Research and an adjunct professor at Duke University Medical Center and Northwestern University Medical School, decided to investigate the relationship between religious commitment and mental or physical health. He discovered little research on the topic, but from the scientific studies he did find, as well as from the research that he and his colleagues eventually conducted, Larson was able to determine that religion significantly influenced health.

One study showed that elderly women with hip fractures recovered sooner and were less depressed if they happened to be religious. Other studies found that people with no interest in religion had the highest mortality rates. Furthermore, the research indicated that people who attended religious services regularly were less likely to abuse alcohol or other drugs, and rarely committed suicide.

Today, due to the research that Larson and others have conducted, the "faith factor" can no longer be ignored. Several medical schools are now actually offering courses on the role of spirituality in medicine. The main trailblazer in this area is Dr. Herbert Benson, associate professor at the Mind-Body Medical Institute at Harvard Medical School and chief of the Division of Behavioral Medicine at Deaconess Hospital. Benson is renowned for his research validating mind-body interactions. For twenty-five years, he has systematically studied how the mind affects the body in measurable ways.

When his research began, his primary intention was to determine if mind-body relaxation techniques could counteract stress-induced symptoms and illnesses. Laboratory findings verified that when individuals learned how to focus their minds on a word, phrase, or prayer — repeating the words or sounds over and over so that other intrusive thoughts were disregarded — physiological changes occurred, such as a decrease in metabolism, blood pressure, and heart rate.

Dubbed "the relaxation response" by Benson, it was shown that regular practice of this meditative technique helped alleviate mild and moderate depression, many forms of chronic pain, as well as symptoms of cancer and AIDS. Benson found the therapy worked for ailments caused by stress as well as illnesses that become stressful.

Over the years, though, another benefit to the relaxation response therapy emerged. As stated, the technique requires the repetition of a word, phrase, or sound. It can be a single word such as "love" or "peace," or a phrase from a prayer, or any sound that relaxes the patient. The patient, not the doctor, decides what to use, but after years of observing patients, Benson realized that 80 percent of them chose a prayer.

Benson found himself in the awkward position of helping patients select a prayer from a variety of faiths. He didn't feel comfortable in this role as a doctor and so invited the clergy to join him at Harvard in teaching appropriate prayers. The bridge between religion and medicine at Harvard started to form, but the patients deserve final credit. They told the doctors that when they used the relaxation response technique they began to feel more attuned spiritually. They described the experience as sensing something beyond them, a force, an energy, a God.

"Physicians are trained to respond to scientific data," says Benson. These comments by patients prompted Benson and his colleagues to specifically investigate the healing effects of spirituality. They then found that patients who had strong spiritual beliefs had fewer medical complaints. "My thoughts have evolved to the point where I see how important belief is and ultimately how important belief in God is," he says.

This research persuaded Benson that doctors need to pay more attention to the relationship between spirituality and healing. "The weight of the evidence has brought us to this point, but it had to be science-based because otherwise you open the door to quacks and charlatans," he says.

"There is a metaphor I like to use," he replies, when asked where faith fits into the routine treatment of patients. "Our overall health and well-being is akin to a three-legged stool. One leg is pharmaceuticals, another leg is surgery and medical procedures, and the third leg is self-care."

It is the third leg that has been largely ignored. And yes, Benson places faith under self-care. The latest research indicates that people need to pay more attention to preventive measures, he says, and taking care of one's spiritual health appears to be as important as nutrition, exercise, and stress-management.

THE POWER OF PRAYER

Benson's work raises the issue of whether prayer, by itself, can heal. The best-known study on prayer was conducted by Randolph Byrd in the early 1980s. As a cardiologist at the San

Francisco General Hospital, Byrd organized a double-blind study of nearly 400 patients in the coronary care unit. Catholic and Protestant prayer groups throughout the United States were asked to pray for some of these patients. This study found that the patients who had been prayed for required fewer antibiotics and had fewer cardiac arrests and deaths.

Since then several other research projects on prayer have also shown promising results. At the California Pacific Medical Center in San Francisco, psychiatrist Elisabeth Targ and psychologist Fred Sicher conducted a double-blind clinical study, based on a successful pilot study, to examine if prayer or psychic healing could help patients with advanced AIDS. Healers from all denominations and a variety of healing traditions participated in the studies. Each day, for a period of ten weeks, the patients received healing messages from ten different healers located throughout the United States. Some prayed in a traditional manner for the patients, while others tried to affect the patients through their own positive thoughts. Because these were double-blind studies, neither the patients nor the investigators knew who was receiving the healing and who the traditional treatment. The results were extremely positive. The patients who received the healing showed improved health compared to the control group, required fewer doctor visits and hospital days, and also had significantly less emotional distress. "We believe," stated the researchers, "this is an important area for further investigation, and has the potential to be developed toward useful clinical application."

"There has been a history in science of simply refusing to look at things outside the dominant paradigm," says Targ. "I feel medical scientists have an ethical obligation to study these areas even if we don't know why they work. In fact, many people tell me they are excited that this research into prayer and distant healing is finally being done by mainstream institutions. We are hoping more laboratories will replicate this research. No one study is definitive, but what our studies have shown is that this is an important area for further research."

Targ comes from a family of pioneers in the field of consciousness. Her father, physicist Russell Targ, helped develop the laser, but is even better known for his investigations into remote viewing, the psychic ability to describe environments and activities at a distance. Russell Targ's research, conducted at the Stanford Research Institute, was backed by the CIA and several government agencies during the 1970s and 1980s. And his findings were published in some of the most prestigious scientific journals throughout the world. For the last three decades, hundreds of experiments have presented evidence of psychic abilities. "No informed person at this point can doubt the reality of remote viewing and other psychic abilities," says Russell Targ. "I think there is an important spiritual message in our work, for our findings show we are all connected."

Elizabeth Targ is specifically interested in this research's implications for healing. "The fact that remote viewing works basically shows us that what happens elsewhere can affect us internally," she says. "It helps us understand how healing could occur."

The studies on prayer and distant healing at the California Pacific Medical Center were partially funded by the Institute of Noetic Sciences (IONS), a nonprofit research and educational institution that provides seed grants for leading-edge scientific and scholarly research. (This author is the editor of the Institute's magazine *Connections*.) As IONS director of research, Marilyn Schlitz has conducted many experiments on healing and intentionality — where one person intentionally tries to affect another person's physiology at a distance.

"The most profound implications of the work are at the societal level," writes Schlitz. "These data support the idea that we are interconnected at a level that has yet to be fully recognized by Western science and that is very far from being integrated into our worldview. If my intentions can influence the physiology of a distant person, if your thoughts can be incorporated into mine, not just in clinical settings but everywhere, it requires that we be more thoughtful and responsible not only for our actions but for the ways in which we think about and interact with other people. It is important to recognize that we are on a frontier, that we are in the process of exploration, that there are many more questions than we have answers for. But that is the thrill of it. The real challenge that faces us is how to learn more about the nature of the human condition and how we can create ourselves as fuller and more complete human beings."

SPONTANEOUS AND MIRACULOUS HEALINGS

The connections between intentionality, spirituality, and healing might explain the phenomena of unexplained reversals of illness, but this subject is also difficult to research. When patients recover unexpectedly from serious illnesses, their cases are often tucked away in the medical literature and dismissed as medical oddities. However, in this easy-to-access information age it is now possible to track these spontaneous remissions, and the phenomena are not as rare as once thought. The Institute of Noetic Sciences has the largest known database on remissions. They have assembled over 4,000 well-documented cases from over 800 medical journals worldwide.

Some people confuse spontaneous remissions with "miraculous" healings, but the one place where miracles are studied — the famous healing shrine at Lourdes, in southwest France — makes a clear distinction between spontaneous and miraculous. More than four million pilgrims visit Lourdes every year. People claiming to have been cured at Lourdes have to produce medical documentation of their illness so it can be officially studied. The Catholic Church discounts any case that looks like spontaneous remission because, in their opinion, spontaneous cures can be activated by the body's own self-restorative powers. To qualify as a miracle, the healing must not only be medically and scientifically inexplicable but instantaneous or sudden (over a few days). Cases are rejected if medical treatment has been given that could induce a cure; the cure must also be complete and permanent.

Since 1858, there have been more than 6,000 claims of miraculous healings, but after an exhaustive investigation of each case by the Medical Bureau at Lourdes and an International Medical Committee of doctors and various specialists, just over sixty miracles have been authenticated and recognized by the Catholic Church. Nevertheless, under these strict standards, the figure is sixty and growing!

Whether one believes a cure is caused by God, or by some extraordinary human healing ability, this area deserves more exploration. Here's one story that shows the dynamics involved in an inexplicable healing, particularly the dynamics of the human heart and spirit.

In the 1960s Rita Klaus was a nun, leading a fairly rigorous life. She rose at 5 A.M., spent two hours in chapel, went on to teach for seven hours, and then in the evening did farm work to help supply the convent's food. She often felt fatigued, which might be considered normal under the circumstances, but when she temporarily lost her vision, not just once but on three occasions, she made an appointment with a neurologist. After examining her, the neurologist said he suspected multiple sclerosis (M.S.), although he couldn't make a definite diagnosis because the illness was in its early stages.

For the next couple of years Rita was not seriously afflicted, but in 1965, while she was recovering from a bad case of flu, she attempted to get out of bed one morning and collapsed on the floor. She spent three months in a hospital and was again diagnosed as having M.S. This time the doctors bluntly told her that they felt religious life was too strenuous for her. Reluctantly, Rita left the convent and accepted a job in special education. As the years went by, and no further symptoms appeared, Rita convinced herself that the initial diagnosis of M.S. was wrong. She buried her doubts and fears to such an extent that when she got married she did not tell her husband her medical history.

Within four years Rita had three children, but after the last one was born she did not recover her strength. Once again, her vision became blurred. One day, as she was holding her three-month-old baby, the child dropped out of her arms; Rita's right hand had gone completely numb. The baby was unharmed, but Rita's problems became more acute. She eventually lost control of her bladder, and her legs became paralyzed. Rita was rushed to the hospital where she underwent several tests, including a spinal tap that determined she had a progressive form of M.S.

Rita was the oldest of six children of Irish Catholic parents. Ron, her husband, was a German Lutheran. Despite religious and cultural differences, their marriage was a good one, but on the night Rita told her husband she had deceived him by not revealing her past problems with M.S., he stood up and walked out of the room yelling, "I want a divorce."

"Later that night he came back," remembers Rita. "I was waiting for him. He said, 'God knows, I'm not a very strong person, and heaven knows, I'm not a saint, but we will try. We will try.'"

Rita's story is about being human and making mistakes just as much as it is about being sick and becoming well. By her own admission, she was not one of those disabled people you meet who shows great patience. She slipped into a deep depression, refused to do her physical therapy, refused to go out of the house. She was angry at everything and everyone, including God. "My only prayer to God was, 'Why did you do this? You can't be a loving God if you let this happen.'"

The paralysis crept from her legs up into her thighs. Her hip became dislocated, and because of the misalignment in her body, the doctors had to reposition her right kneecap, turning it toward the left leg. She wore steel braces and could only walk a few steps with the aid of crutches. Most of the time she lived in a wheel-chair.

In 1986, a friend invited her to a laying-on-of-hands healing service at a nearby church. Rita refused, saying she disapproved of such healers. The friend kept trying to persuade her to attend the healing mass, and on the day of the service even her husband said, "Why don't you go? We've been to every doctor and there's nobody who can help you. Is this going to hurt? Go. Do it for me."

So she went. The church was packed, but she found a place near the back, right on the aisle. There were several priests conducting the service, and as they began to walk up the aisle, one spotted her. Without warning she found herself being held by this priest in an effusive bear hug. The uninvited hug made Rita embarrassed, but as the priest continued to hold her, she recalls that all at once she felt as if she were being hugged by God. "A great peace came, and I found myself praying my first real prayer in years," she remembers. "I had this awareness of being loved tremendously, just tremendously."

She returned home after the healing service not healed in body but in spirit. "My husband hoped I would come home walking; instead I came home singing," she says.

Her physical body continued to deteriorate, but emotionally and spiritually she had never been better. She went back to teaching and felt a continuing sense of joy.

A few months later, she read an article about the alleged appearances of the Virgin Mary and reports of miraculous healings in the village of Medjugorje in Yugoslavia. A short time after reading this article, while getting ready for bed one night, she heard a voice say, "Why don't you ask?" And so Rita offered a prayer, with this request, "Dear Mary, my mother, Queen of Peace, whom I believe is appearing to the children at Medjugorje, please ask your son to heal me in any way I need to be healed. I know your son has said that if you have faith and you say to the mountains move, that they will move. I believe. Please help my unbelief."

As she finished the prayer, Rita says she felt as if a surge of electricity had pierced her body. The next morning she went to the college where she was taking a scripture course. While in class, she realized she could wiggle her toes. When she got home that afternoon, she removed her braces and looked down at her legs. She was astounded to see that her deformed right kneecap was straight.

Her family was not home yet, so she started to walk around the house on her crutches, still thinking she needed them. Suddenly she saw her whole life in review, from her childhood to the prayer she had said the night before. From that moment, she knew she was completely cured. She put the crutches away and ran up the stairs to the second floor. She ran outside, and she kept running, screaming to the sky, "Thank you God, thank you Blessed Mother."

Rita was later examined by several doctors who confirmed she had fully recovered. Spontaneous remission from M.S. is possible, but Rita's illness was advanced, and doctors cannot explain how deformed bones were healed or how Rita could immediately walk, run, and use muscles that had been atrophied for years.

Rita has no doubt her cure was miraculous, but she believes her physical healing would not have occurred if she had not first been healed spiritually. "Before the physical healing I couldn't walk," she says. "After the physical healing I could walk. But my real healing was the spiritual one."

COMPLEMENTARY MEDICINE AND WHOLENESS

This type of miraculous healing seems unbelievable, but these stories, along with increasing research, are beginning to dramatically change perceptions in medicine. Consider developments in Britain. Throughout most of his life British businessman Denis Haviland had no interest in spiritual healing. If anything, he was highly skeptical of the phenomenon. But his opinion changed completely through experience. As a young man Haviland broke his leg so severely while skiing that doctors considered amputating it. Although his leg was saved, he suffered excruciating pain for years and could only walk with the aid of a cane.

His doctor finally suggested that Haviland undergo a hip replacement operation, but just before the surgery was scheduled, Haviland met a spiritual healer. After many sessions with this healer, his hip joint fused, making surgery unnecessary.

This experience convinced Haviland that spiritual healing should not be renounced so readily by skeptics. His next move was ingeniously straightforward. Knowing the potential for quackery was a top concern, Haviland decided to try to regulate spiritual healers. He persuaded the different spiritual and lay healing associations in Britain to find common ground under one group called the Confederation of Healing Organisations. Then he asked several well-known doctors to specify the dangers they perceived in spiritual healing and how this form of healing could be used more constructively. From the answers he received, a binding Code of Conduct was formed. Doctors were concerned about the possibility of healers misdiagnosing illnesses, and so the code stipulates that healers cannot give a diagnosis or suggest medical treatment;

they must advise patients to see a doctor. The list of restrictions continues, paring down the basic purpose of healers: They can only offer healing through their hands or at a distance by prayer and thought transference.

Several thousand healers now belong to the Confederation of Healing Organisations and follow its obligatory Code of Conduct. One sign that this code has transformed spiritual and lay healing into a standard therapy in Britain is that these healers are covered by a comprehensive insurance policy. Without the threat of liability, several hospitals with AIDS and cancer wards now work with healers.

Haviland also helped form the British Complementary Medical Association. In Britain, the term "complementary medicine" is more widely used than "alternative medicine," emphasizing that the goal is not to turn patients away from traditional care. Whereas traditional medicine concentrates on the physical problem, many complementary therapies focus more on the emotional, social, and spiritual aspects of an illness. Together they treat the whole person. Such techniques as acupuncture, homeopathy, osteopathy, and Qigong exercises have slipped into mainstream medical practice in Britain.

Meanwhile, back in the United States, the National Institutes of Health has established the Office of Alternative Medicine, and HMOs are starting to offer patients acupuncture treatments and other nontraditional therapies. The use of imagery for medical problems is especially popular, and the Academy for Guided Imagery in California provides a special certification program for health professionals in imagery techniques.

Martin Rossman is a physician and codirector of this academy. Ample documentation exists, he says, to show that imagery can relieve chronic pain, alter blood flow, and stimulate other changes that we once believed couldn't be controlled consciously. "As a culture," says Rossman, "we are becoming much more aware of the importance of imagery as a way of processing information. Imagery is a central organizing mechanism, and is a relatively direct representation of what goes on in us unconsciously. It can be used for mundane and practical purposes, or it can be used to connect us with our highest spiritual selves."

Psychologist Jeanne Achterberg is well-known for her research into the application of imagery for catastrophic illness. She has observed, however, that choosing a healing method is like choosing anything in life: We are swayed by personal beliefs and experiences. To Achterberg, *belief* is the key word. She has seen patients recover unexpectedly from catastrophic illnesses by adopting special diets they passionately believe in, or by concentrating on imagery, or by relying totally on Western medicine and doing nothing, or nothing consciously, to encourage their self-healing capabilities.

Says Achterberg, "I'm not dogmatic about many things, because I've been proven wrong too often, but I am dogmatic about this: There is no one thing that's going to heal us. The best advice I can give is to see where your belief system hangs and put your energy there."

THE INTENT TO HEAL APPLIED TO EVERYDAY LIVING

Attachment to a belief system does involve one vital component: intention. Intention is crucial in a healing technique called Therapeutic Touch — another example of how the act of healing can invoke the best in us. Therapeutic Touch was derived from the ancient practice of laying on of hands, but the modern method, which was developed by Dora Kunz, a healer, and Dolores Krieger, Ph.D., a professor of nursing, has no religious context. The technique is based on the notion that the human being is an open energy system and therefore it is possible for individuals to fine-tune their own energy to help themselves, or transfer energy to help others.

To demonstrate that anyone can transfer healing energy if he or she wishes to, Krieger began teaching Therapeutic Touch to registered nurses in the United States as far back as 1972. Since then, this technique has been taught in more than 100 universities and colleges in the United States, and in over 70 foreign countries. Dr. Krieger has personally taught Therapeutic Touch to more than 43,000 professionals in the health field.

Many doctoral dissertations have been completed on Therapeutic Touch and scientific research has substantiated that this technique can, at the very least, greatly reduce anxiety and pain. Dr. Janet Quinn, at the University of Colorado Health Sciences Center School of Nursing, conducted one revealing study with a group of nurses who were asked to apply Therapeutic Touch to patients in a cardiovascular unit. These nurses moved their hands over the patients' bodies, deliberately directing energy, and completely focusing their consciousness on the act of healing.

In the same experiment, other nurses were instructed to mimic the treatments. The mimic group duplicated the hand movements, but their intention was not to heal; they gave no real sense of caring or compassion. While imitating the hand movements, these nurses simply counted backwards from 100.

The findings of this study, and other studies that have replicated it, reveal there was little or no effect on patients when the treatments were mimicked, but there was a distinct reduction in a patient's emotional state when they were treated by people who intentionally wanted to help them. "Same procedure, different intent, different effects," concludes Quinn. Significantly, she feels the implications of these research findings about the role of intention and its effects "extend beyond the care-giving context into the dimensions of everyday living."

"Thus, the old adage that it is not what you say but how you say it can also be applied to how we give care," she writes. "It is not what you do, it is the intent with which you do it that determines the outcome. How many ordinary events in day-to-day life are also governed by this axiom?"

Quinn asks, "What would the effect be if when we said to a friend, 'It's very good to see you,' we really focused our attention on that friend and 'sent' the loving thought or 'energy' that our words attempt to communicate? Can you begin to see the healing that could take place? Can you begin to realize that we are all potentially healers? That we have only to pay attention, to make the intention to be helpful?"

A BROADER VIEW OF HEALING

Many of the healing techniques and therapies discussed here can, in their own way, indelibly affect a person — depending upon how they are applied and interwoven into that person's way of life.

"The hallmark of Therapeutic Touch," says Krieger, "is that you're tapping into the higher orders of self. You begin by centering your consciousness and you stay centered through the entire healing process, so you're pulling from these farther reaches of consciousness. This is what makes the difference. You really have to get in touch with the deep places within yourself, and there is just no way you can practice it without it changing your lifestyle and also your worldview."

When people think of transformational experiences that alter lifestyles and views of truth, they tend to focus on the negative: wars, deaths, divorces — anything that crushes the human life or spirit. Yet Krieger and others are telling us that it is the act of healing, not the act of destruction, that reshapes us.

The word heal, whole, and holy all stem from the same root,

and they share a partnership in practice as well. As we examine different life-affirming steps that people take to overcome an illness, common elements emerge that promote the journey toward wholeness: expansive hearts, inner peace, a sense of purpose and meaning, and often a sense of *connection* to a God or higher source.

To Rachel Naomi Remen, who has witnessed as a doctor again and again how an illness can transform an individual, healing is ultimately a sacred act: "It's about uncovering, recovering, discovering the innate wholeness in ourselves and in the world."

Finally, one aspect of healing is self-evident: Regardless of the healing method chosen, it is the *process* of healing that delivers the magical results. Embedded in the process is the opportunity to improve — improve the body, improve oneself, improve life.

Thus health becomes a fundamental beginning for the journey toward a new culture. In many ways health professionals are pioneers in cultivating the best in human nature; and their approaches go far beyond health care.

Dr. Leonard Duhl, professor of city planning and public health at the University of California, Berkeley, makes this unsettling comparison: "You can't live with cancer in the liver and have the rest of you healthy, just as you can't live with homeless or hungry people in one corner and have the rest of the city fine."

Healing appears to be a catalyst for change. It is a never-ending circle that starts within, manifests in the body, and embraces all that is around us.

CHAPTER FOUR

Working to Benefit Society

Work is about making money. People obviously work for many other reasons, but the official economy only considers you employed if you pocket a paycheck. People who volunteer or work at home taking care of their children are not counted as part of the work force because they don't earn anything.

Work is not only about making money to buy food and life's necessities but about securing profits for companies. In a free society a business can make a profit in any legal way they wish. Tobacco companies profit from people addicted to smoking. Corporations can profit from polluting the environment, exploiting workers, or building weapons. For too long a company's responsibility for its own prosperity, and its responsibility to society at large have rarely been considered together.

Today the business world has a split personality. Whether through genuine reform or corporate public relations, one side expresses a sunny image, as corporate leaders stress high standards of ethics, and the advantages of teamwork, cooperation, and working for the common good. The word "soul" even keeps popping up in book titles and articles as authors outline a more ennobling marketplace where workers can find meaningful work that feeds the human spirit.

But the darker side of business is lean and mean. Corporations ruthlessly lay off employees to make more money for stockholders. According to an analysis of Labor Department statistics by the *New York Times*, more than 43 million jobs have been lost since 1979. All types of employees have been affected, from administrators to blue-collar workers, and although most of these workers are finding others jobs, pay and benefits are usually less, while the social price of this job insecurity is yet to be measured.

Jeremy Rifkin's book *The End of Work* warns that as technology replaces people with intelligent machines, fewer workers will be needed to produce goods and services. He writes, "Whether the new technologies free us for a life of increasing leisure or result in massive unemployment and a potential global depression will depend in large part on how each nation addresses the question of productivity advances."

Continually advancing productivity has become a problem in many ways. Societies that pump out more and more goods to create more and more jobs are running up against the realization that our planet has limited resources. We now have to ask ourselves this difficult question: What are we working for? Work that harms society or just gobbles precious resources is being criticized. Working just to make money is no longer enough. The health of society will eventually depend upon how wise we are in reinventing the role of work to benefit the planet and all workers. People need jobs with meaning, jobs that satisfy the human spirit. This chapter, therefore, examines how we can create a better relationship between work and our whole quality of life.

CONNECTING WORK LIFE WITH HOME LIFE

The connection between work and quality of life has a contentious starting point: work-family issues. Futurist Harris Sussman describes this area as the "ecosystem of society, the way home and school and work and family are tied together."

Sussman is a specialist on changes in work and organizational practices, and he contends that the next frontier is the unification of work and family responsibilities. Companies, he says, are realizing they now have to consider parts of a person's life that used to be beyond the scope of work. Such issues as child care, wellness programs, benefits, employee relations, community relations, or telecommuting eventually force both employee and employer to address what he calls the *reconciliation* of people's work lives with their personal lives. "All these concerns that didn't seem to be either appropriate or relevant to discuss at work are now central to a person being able to be more fully productive, more holistically engaged in the work they are asked to do," he says.

"What's so difficult about work-family issues is that the solutions require a change in the work ethic as we have known it," he acknowledges. "Work-family is about renegotiating our work ethic and the terms of the social order that have been in place for centuries."

A nonprofit organization called the Families and Work Institute, which conducts research on business, government, and community efforts to help employees balance job and family responsibilities, compiled these statistics to detail our complex lives: Eighty-six percent of U.S. workers live in households where they have some degree of day-to-day family responsibility. Forty-six percent have children under eighteen at home, and about thirteen percent take care of an elderly relative. Forty-eight percent expect to have elder-care responsibilities within the next five years.

With both parents working, balancing home life and work life is a precarious juggling act for both men and women, and when home life falls apart, the repercussions appear in absenteeism from work, skyrocketing divorce rates, child abuse, and child neglect. Caring for our children produces more passionate rhetoric and promises than most subjects, but after all is said and done (or rather, not done) the United States doesn't have a formal government policy on how to meet the needs of families. Some corporations offer on-site day-care programs, but as Sussman states, "We've got 20,000 social policies being formulated by 20,000 employers, so it is a real hodgepodge of policies and practices with the employee being stigmatized for having needs in the first place."

The present climate of downsizing adds an awkward complication because employees often fear they will lose their jobs if they ask for personal considerations. Dana Friedman, senior vice president of Corporate Family Solutions, an organization specializing in work-life consulting, observes, "There is no question that the 'lean and mean' phenomenon is going against the grain of what employees increasingly desire, which is an improved quality of life."

If anything, as workers are laid off, remaining employees shoulder greater responsibilities and longer work hours, with home life as the natural casualty. However, says Friedman, when an MIT research team visited one company where employees had worked several nights in a row to finish a proposal, they noticed more sensitivity toward the work-family time crunch. "The employees were congratulating themselves," she says, "when all of a sudden the manager said, 'Wait a minute, what is wrong with this picture? I am not so sure we should be celebrating. We have stayed up for the last four nights doing this work, but is it our best work? I am sure you haven't seen your families in about a week, and you are going to be useless to me for the next two weeks. So why are we congratulating ourselves? Maybe the real issue here is that we didn't plan well.'"

Business leaders must get to the point, says Friedman, where they stop to ask whether their work schedules are good for business *and* for families. "In most cases, the answer is no to both."

Conversely, research conducted by the Families and Work Institute found that when companies are responsive to family concerns and introduce practical work-family policies, their employees are far more committed to helping the organization succeed. Ultimately everybody benefits.

Merck and Company is an international pharmaceutical conglomerate that employs about 55,000 people. Over the years Merck has introduced many programs to help families, such as on-site day-care centers, unpaid parental leave for men and women, and fitness programs. Even so, when their managers and employees were asked for feedback on company policies, work-life issues were identified as an area where the company needs to keep improving.

Work-life concerns cannot necessarily be solved by simply adding more programs. Merck, and other companies, struggle with how to streamline jobs and eliminate unnecessary tasks in order to make the working environment not only more satisfying but more flexible. In particular, old bureaucratic methods of controlling workers by keeping them in plain sight is no longer necessary or welcome. Technology allows people to interact with one another across distances, paving the way for independence and also for more trust between managers and employees.

For instance, Dr. Susan Aiello, the editor of the *Merck Veterinary Manual* moved to Canada when her husband was offered a new job. Instead of leaving her position, an arrangement was made so she could work full-time from her home. She stays in contact with her colleagues via the telephone, e-mail, and faxes. Later, she moved back to the United States, but remains in a different state than the company's headquarters.

"Work is now place-free and time-free," says Harris Sussman. "We're in the middle of a remarkable structural transition from one way in which work has been done for several generations to a new way that is just emerging."

TIME FOR A CHANGE

Meanwhile, the ticking bomb is time. It is has become normal for executives to work over sixty hours a week. Janet McLaughlin, the director of Human Resources Effectiveness and Education for Corning, works part-time, but that still means about forty hours a week. "It is part-time compared to my peers," she says, laughing. Yet she is grateful for a flexible schedule. Twice a week she leaves her office at 1:30 P.M. to pick up her children from school, and when necessary, works nights and weekends on her home computer. "I have received five promotions over a twelve-year period," says McLaughlin. "My part-time status has never been a concern."

More of a concern is that many full-time professionals feel obligated to routinely work extraordinary hours in order to make an impression, keep up with the competition, or simply keep their jobs. Closely tied to work-family issues is a movement to shorten these hours. Throughout this book, people have stressed the importance of leading a whole, balanced life, and the shorter work-time movement is one more piece that needs to be put in place. At the moment people are running so fast they trip. They have little time to relax, enjoy their family, participate in neighborhood activities, volunteer in the community, or expand the heart and spirit in all the ways that finally make life worthwhile.

Barbara Brandt is an organizer for the Shorter Work-Time Group, which is trying to raise public consciousness about what she calls "the devastating effects that overwork is having on our health, our families, and our communities."

She notes that Americans work about 200 hours a year more than Europeans. However, we don't work as much as the Japanese, who have even coined a new word — *Karoshi* — which means death from overwork. In a world economy based on competitiveness, says Brandt, we have developed the trap of pitting one country against another to keep ahead. But gaining the competitive edge becomes a dangerous game when enslaving ourselves to our jobs erodes our quality of life. In the long run, she urges, the only way any nation can advance is by considering not just economic curves but the well-being of all citizens.

American leaders, she asserts, have basically ignored the broad social repercussions of a workaholic society, where lack of time with family, friends, and civic groups has resulted in the breakdown of both family life and the community spirit. "We need to publicly discuss this issue by asking what kind of society do we want to have?" she says.

One country that has taken a significant step toward this discourse is Canada. In 1994, the Canadian Minister of Human Resources and Development appointed a committee to study whether shorter hours and a more equitable distribution of work could improve job prospects, and improve the balance between family and work responsibilities.

The results of this study were encouraging. Arthur Donner, an economist who chaired the committee, noted this dichotomy: Due to downsizing, people who have jobs are expected to work longer, but part-time work is growing faster than full-time work. Many working part-time want to work full-time because they are not earning enough money, and those working long hours want shorter ones. Add to this the fact that there are not enough jobs for everyone.

The win-win solution, says Donner, is to make full-time work less arduous and part-time work more attractive. "In practical terms," states the committee's report, "this implies reduced working hours for some people currently working long hours, increasing working time for others who are working fewer hours than they want to, as well as the creation of some new jobs for individuals who are currently unemployed."

A reduction in hours usually means a reduction in pay, but, explains Donner, the ultimate payoff to society is worthwhile. A significantly shorter work week — a four-day week is one option — could dramatically boost employment. The total government budgetary picture would then improve because as unemployment drops, the welfare burden decreases.

"My personal feeling," concludes this economist, "is we're really moving into a world where there aren't going to be enough jobs. We have got to have some form of work redistribution. Besides, whatever happened to all the talk in the early '50s that the standard work week by the year 2000 would be twenty hours a week? Whatever happened to the leisure society?"

A GENUINE PICTURE OF THE ECONOMY

The work ethic is so strong in American culture that leisure is often equated with laziness. But the main concern is that if workers produce less, the economic health of a society could be threatened. Reassuringly, the Canadian study found that the size of the economy, as measured by the gross domestic product (GDP), would hardly be affected by a reduction in work time.

In any country, economic growth is the golden gauge that determines whether a society is thriving or deteriorating. You can't stop growth, people argue. You can't stop progress. "Growth" and "progress" are our most powerful work-and-money magnets. However, we have clung to them for so long we have almost forgotten why we have become so attached.

"The question is what do we really mean by progress?" challenges Ted Halstead, who is the founder and board member of a United States think tank appropriately named Redefining Progress. In trying to redefine how a country measures economic and social progress, this organization has devised an alternative economic measurement that reflects a national movement to alter how economic policy is shaped.

During World War II, the gross national product (GNP) was developed as a way to plan and measure the war production effort. This indicator, now referred to as gross domestic product (GDP), continues to measure production. When the GDP rises, politicians and policymakers cheer. It is assumed that the more goods and services we buy and sell, the better off we are as a society. That is progress. Or is it?

Halstead and his colleagues contend that the GDP is highly misleading as an indicator of economic health because only the gross is measured; there are no deductions for costs and losses, and no distinction made between productive or destructive activities. It would be a ludicrous way to run a business, and yet that is the way we run a country. For instance, crime, divorce, and natural disasters force people to spend money, and therefore the GDP regards a costly divorce or the construction of another prison as economic gain. Under this scorecard, the breakdown of the social structure is to our benefit because money is being exchanged. Similarly, when ancient forests are cut down, timber sales are recorded as income, rather than a depreciation of an asset.

Pollution and ecological damage also increase economic activity through the billions of dollars required to combat environmental degradation.

It is an accounting system stuck in addition, rarely subtracting for social, emotional, or ecological costs. Criticism of the system is not new. In 1968, Robert Kennedy stated, "The GNP counts air pollution and cigarette advertising and ambulances to clear our highways of carnage. . . . Yet the gross national product does not allow for the health of our children, the quality of their education, or the joy of their play. . . . It measures neither our wit nor our courage; neither our wisdom nor our learning; neither our compassion or our devotion to our country; it measures everything, in short, except that which makes life worthwhile."

What has compassion, wit, or quality of education to do with economics? Absolutely nothing if we stick to our present way of compartmentalizing all human activity. In this segregated system, progress is counted purely in financial terms and quality of life is left off the balance sheet. Official figures discount activities that in reality are priceless, such as volunteer work, household tasks, and the social benefits of caring for children and the elderly.

But at Redefining Progress they reason that "a parent raising a child is engaged in an economic activity just as surely as someone working in a factory, store, or office." This work, they add, is more essential to the survival and health of our society than many office or factory jobs and yet the task of nurturing children is often valued only in retrospect, after we suffer the consequences of neglecting them.

"The whole mindset in Western society," says Halstead, "is that if something is not part of the market economy, if it is not paid for in some financial transaction, then it is worthless, but a very wide range of things bring tremendous value to any society. We need to incorporate them into our definition of progress."

Redefining Progress has developed what they call the "genuine progress indicator" (GPI), a concept based on the pioneering work of economist Herman Daly and theologian John Cobb. Instead of relying on gross figures, the GPI looks at the net, subtracting such factors as the loss of leisure, crime-related costs, or resource depletion, while at the same time calculating the value of child-care, household work, and volunteerism.

The GPI still measures market-based transactions, but its intent is to evaluate the whole picture — whether we are succeeding or failing in areas that matter the most to us as a nation. To move from theory to practical application, Redefining Progress produced a chart comparing the gross domestic product with the genuine progress indicator from 1950 to the present. The findings showed that although the GDP rose steadily throughout most of these years, the GPI documented a steady decline in the health of the economy since the '70s. The estimated dollar value of social and environmental costs rose faster than the benefits of economic growth. Such a course is clearly not sustainable.

One of the solutions proposed by Redefining Progress is to redesign the tax code and incentive structure. They are not against growth, just against growth being an end in itself. "Right now," explains Halstead, "we tax human labor and do not tax the use of natural resources to any significant extent. So basically we have an incentive structure where companies are encouraged to get rid of human labor in favor of machines, because energy is cheap and humans are expensive. What we are suggesting is to completely flip-flop the incentive structure to make it more attractive for companies to fund human labor. It will bring us less of what we don't want — the depletion of natural resources — and more of what we do want."

These concepts are just beginning steps. None of this will happen easily, quickly, or without running into opposition.

France and Australia, however, are already discussing new ways to measure their economies, and in the United States, over 400 economists signed a declaration saying that GDP is "both inadequate and misleading as a measure of true prosperity." Many have joined this call for better ways to measure the health of the whole economy, including Herbert Simon, a Nobel economics laureate; Oscar Arias, former president of Costa Rica and Nobel Peace Prize recipient; Ted Turner, the media magnate; and Maurice Strong at the World Bank, who is also special advisor to the secretary general at the United Nations.

For years, obsolete and false economic indicators have led policymakers astray. As they assert at Redefining Progress, "Although the public realizes that we face real social and ecological problems, they do not recognize these problems as the interconnected symptoms of misguided economic growth."

THE MATTER WITH MATERIALISM

Equating economic prosperity with material consumption has been the American way of life. America is not only the land of opportunity but the land of abundance. Success is measured in material achievements — the big house stuffed with stuff. The craving for material things, to keep buying and buying, is one reason why people work so hard. Lately, though, criticism of our materialistic society has begun to rise from a low rumble to an audible challenge.

Businesses can't afford to turn a deaf ear to the discussions now taking place about how excessive materialism is connected to social decay. As we cross the line from the need to greed, our shopping frenzy had skewed our values and priorities, and placed many in serious debt. A nationwide random survey conducted by the Harwood Group, a public issues research and innovations firm, showed that 82 percent of those surveyed felt that most people buy and consume far more than they need.

"What we're tackling," reflects Richard Harwood, president of the Harwood Group, "is a strong belief among a lot of people that our individual lives and the country itself are off track. We have become so enamored with material goods, and keeping up with the Joneses, that it is damaging our spiritual well-being, our sense of community, and our belief that we're connected to one another beyond a market-based approach. We have misplaced many of the values that need to guide a democratic and responsible society."

But while surveys have found that people's deepest aspirations are nonmaterial, the desire for financial security is as strong as ever. The struggle right now, says Harwood, is to reestablish a sense of balance in society. We're entering a new era where values, norms, and relationships are being reshuffled. A great part of this reshuffling relates to work and the economy, but Harwood cautions, it is too easy, and too risky, for politicians and activists to claim they have "the answer" to societal problems. "What is needed," he says, "is a process of discovery."

Harwood's own business is a sign of the times. Having worked for a number of years on political campaigns, he knows only too well how political organizations can manipulate and divide people through surveys and orchestrated public relations. He set out to see if was possible to create an organization that could facilitate effective social change by researching and framing public issues in a way that invites open discussion, where people from all political parties and economic positions can work with one another, rather than against each other.

Without a doubt, people are crying out for a serious give-and-take exchange of ideas. A couple of years ago the Merck Family Fund sponsored a conference that pulled together individuals who don't normally meet under one roof: business representatives, religious leaders, environmental activists, consumer group representatives, government officials, and academicians. For three days they debated, sometimes in heated dialogue, why the materialistic "American Dream" is becoming nightmarish. Again, the talk dwelled on unsustainable consumption patterns; the United States represents less than 5 percent of the world's population but consumes nearly 30 percent of the planet's resources.

The conference didn't provide a blueprint for action, but it did give birth to an organization called The Center for a New American Dream, with the intent of keeping the conversation going through a network of individuals and groups who want to work toward a new future. The Center for a New American Dream now acts as a catalyst and a clearinghouse; people can get information about what others are doing on a political, professional, or personal level, and draw inspiration and strength from these efforts.

One person who has already inspired others to change the way they view work, money, and shopping sprees is Vicki Robin. She is coauthor, with Joe Dominguez, of the national bestseller *Your Money or Your Life*. Robin now heads the New Road Map Foundation, an all-volunteer educational and charitable organization committed to helping people transform their lives by transforming their relationship with money.

"People see their financial life as a separate department," says Robin. "They think that their behavior with money doesn't leak into home life, into their spiritual life, but it does. Ours is a whole-person approach, which gives people the freedom to say, 'I have only a certain number of years to live and I am going to make the best of them. I am going to live to my highest and I am going to handle my money in such a way that I can do that.'"

Although this sounds idealistic, millions of Americans have already chosen to scale back their spending habits. They're saving more and refusing to sell their soul for a lifestyle of material status.

When asked what matters most to them they say their wealth lies in personal relationships. The Trends Research Institute in New York predicts that this movement, known as Voluntary Simplicity, will continue to be one of the top trends throughout the '90s and well into the new millennium. They estimate that in a few years about 15 percent of the baby boomers will have simplified their lifestyles, a substantial figure when one realizes that a decade ago this movement was hardly detectable.

Reducing consumption voluntarily is different from having to cut back due to a divorce, loss of a job, or any economic problem. Yet the Trends Research Institute also found that even when people are forced to simplify their lifestyles, they eventually gain greater control over their lives and start to enjoy their reduced pace.

But where does running a business and making a profit fit into this picture? Kevin Sweeney, the communications director of Patagonia, the outdoor clothing company, acknowledges, "I attend meetings where environmentalists talk about the problems of overconsumption, but we are a consumer products company. We are proud of what we do, and when people buy our things, we make money."

What makes Patagonia stand out in the crowd, however, is that they are willing to go out of their way to respond to the interlocking challenges of economic stability and environmental sustainability. In 1996, for example, they made a commitment to use only organically grown cotton.

As for the sensitive subject of customers buying fewer products, which immediately triggers fear of higher unemployment, Sweeney suggests that if companies focus on quality rather than quantity, it could bolster jobs, not threaten them. "If you grow produce organically it requires more labor, but you are putting money into people, not chemicals," he says. "It also takes a lot of labor to produce wonderful handcrafted garments. Ideally, the goal would be to make products that last a long time, so people can buy fewer things. And then the company isn't extracting as many resources from the earth."

Patagonia, he emphasizes, doesn't pretend to have resolved the daunting question of how to operate a business so the company thrives without exploiting the environment or its employees. "We keep asking for help," he says. "When you understand how deep many of these problems are, you acquire humility."

Shortly after Patagonia announced that they had switched to organic cotton, an investment bank approached this private company and tried to persuade them to go public. "They told us," recalls Sweeney, "that people love your environmental stance. Then they said we don't want you to change, but the only thing you have to do is promise to grow at least 10 percent a year. We said no, we're going to stay private. We realized if we went public under those conditions we would be a different company."

The pressure of rapid growth, and the pressure of *having* to grow, says Sweeney, can completely change how a company operates, because decisions too readily succumb to the all-powerful bottom line. "If the corporate world ever grapples with the issue of profit — What is the right kind of profit? What is fair? — that would be genuinely radical."

INVESTING WITH A CONSCIENCE

Indeed, corporate profits and earnings from investments are the sacred cows. They are rarely evaluated to see how the profits-performance connection influences corporate actions. John Harrington, an investment advisor who helped pioneer the concept of investing with a conscience, concedes this reality. "Even investment managers like myself are under the gun every quarter to increase performance," he says. "In the old days, you invested in a company and you stuck with it. Now you are in and out. The major issue is whether or not short-term profits are important for a company. Short-term profits might not equate to long-run profitability. It may be better for a company to underperform in the short run but in the long run be stronger."

On the positive side, there has been a steady increase in the number of people who are deliberately investing in companies with sound social and environmental records. Harrington estimates socially responsible investments are over a trillion-dollar industry. "Of the total capital market you're talking less than ten percent," he says. "Yet that is tremendous, and it is growing by hundreds of millions of dollars a year. If you look back a few years ago it wasn't even one half a percent of the total capital market."

When the flow of capital moves in a certain direction, says Harrington, and when shareholders actively support corporations that are contributing in some way to the well-being of society, these forces not only influence business and political decisions but reverberate through the whole culture.

SHOPPING WITH A SOCIAL CONSCIENCE

You don't have to be an investor to make money work for the benefit of society. You can shop with a social conscience by refusing to buy from companies that are unresponsive to social issues. A great deal of credit for the evolvement of the socially conscious consumer goes to Alice Tepper Marlin, who founded the Council on Economic Priorities (CEP).

Since 1969, CEP has conducted research on how companies, both large and small, respond to environmental and social concerns. When CEP first began examining corporate records in such areas as environmental stewardship, community involvement, and equal employment opportunity, companies were reluctant to disclose information. "None of your business" was the usual business response. Their arrogant posture changed when the public began to realize that corporations weren't detached entities in a society, but an integral main artery, capable of either sustaining or jeopardizing the health of humanity.

"That's made our work much easier," says Marlin. "Now no one questions our basic right to ask questions. Nor do they question the premise that business should be socially responsible. It's almost apple pie."

CEP publishes studies and reports on corporate policies, encouraging consumers to "turn their shopping cart into a vehicle for social change." They also offer a research service called SCREEN for investors, and they present annual Corporate Conscience Awards to American companies, as well as international companies based in Europe and Japan. For example, they honored Pfizer for its Sharing the Care program, which gives medicine to low-income, uninsured patients who might not otherwise receive needed prescriptions. It is the largest pharmaceuticals access program in the United States, administered in partnership with the National Governors' Association and the National Association of Community Health Centers.

On an international level, Fuji Xerox, a joint venture of Fuji Photo Film and Xerox Corporation, received an award for their Social Service Leave Program. Employees can take a leave of six months to two years to work on social welfare projects for local or national institutions, and the company continues to pay their salary.

"These innovative companies," says Tepper Marlin, "have pioneered significant programs that we hope others will emulate."

WHEN THE CONSCIENCE IS WORKING

It isn't difficult to find companies with a heart. However, it also isn't hard to come across companies that harm the environment and show little regard for their employees. During the past few years, a number of university students have signed a voluntary graduation pledge to "investigate and take into account the social and environmental consequences of any job opportunity I consider."

The concept of a graduation pledge began at Humboldt State University in California. Today, Manchester College in Indiana acts as the headquarters for a national campaign to persuade graduating students to follow not only their dreams but their heart and conscience when choosing a job.

Nevertheless, most people inevitably consider salary, security, and status first when taking a job. John Krumboltz is a Stanford University professor of education and psychology who in 1990 was presented with the Leona Tyler Award of the American Psychological Association, the nation's foremost award in the field of counseling psychology. He has given a lot of thought to how people choose their careers, or as he says, whether they choose them at all.

Because jobs are difficult to obtain in today's society, says Krumboltz, many young people readily accept any work opportunity that crosses their path, or they find themselves being pressured by parents and friends to specialize in one area before they have had a chance to explore all options. "Most people stumble from one accident to another," he says, "and many find themselves doing something they don't like, but they continue doing it because they get locked into it. The pay is satisfactory, their mortgage payments are due, and pretty soon they have spent almost a lifetime doing something they hate."

This type of discontentment is a personal as well as societal tragedy, believes Krumboltz. "Here is a decision that affects everything in our future," he says, "not just how we spend eight hours a day, fifty weeks a year — but probably who we're going to marry, the neighborhood in which we live, who our friends are going to be, and how much money we have to spend."

A decision with such far-reaching consequences, adds

Krumboltz, deserves careful study, but courses on life planning are usually run with the leftovers from the academic purse. Overworked school counselors are responsible for too many students and don't have the time to offer comprehensive advice about career choices.

"We're ignoring the most important decision that people face," he says. "There is an implicit assumption that you just fill people's heads with a bunch of facts in school, then turn them loose, and they'll know what to do."

Krumboltz recommends that society place a greater priority on these career decision-making processes. However, he also warns that when people do carefully plan their careers, they still need to remain flexible and open to new opportunities throughout their lives. "You shouldn't plan what you're going to do for the rest of your life at age eighteen. It is not realistic or even desirable."

Krumboltz has one more piece of advice: He would like to see an end to "occupationism," a term he puts in the same category as the other "isms" — racism and sexism. Occupationism, he maintains, is another form of prejudice because individuals are judged by what they do for a living, rather than by their character. Doctors, lawyers, and professors are placed on a prestige pedestal, while too many people look down on car mechanics, sales clerks, and other blue-collar occupations.

"Prestige accrues to those with fancy job titles, not necessarily to those who do good work," Krumboltz says. "I remember well the snide comments that were made in undergraduate school about those members of our class who planned to be teachers. But good teachers make immensely important contributions in our society."

MEANINGFUL WORK

There are many short-sighted ways to categorize people and what they do for a living. Take the career of Kim Marienthal. In the late '60s, while Marienthal was still in high school, he became interested in ecology, particularly in saving trees. He realized that thousands of trees could be preserved if people used multipurpose canvas bags instead of paper. So he made some sample bags, started gathering purchase orders, and then took the purchase orders to a bank and obtained a bank loan. He was in business: the "Save a Tree" business.

Before Marienthal was out of high school he was selling his bags across America to health food stores and food co-ops. His Save a Tree bags paid his way through college and graduate school, but in the early '80s his business slumped and Kim ventured into real estate, a field with a very different social perception. Kim's principles didn't change, only his job, but he is well aware that with his Save a Tree business he was identified as a person who helped the environment. In contrast, when identified with real estate, it is often presumed his business exploits the environment.

"There is absolutely the potential for rape and plunder in the real estate business, as with almost any business," Kim says in response to such pigeonholing. "But I also feel there is equal potential to be environmentally conscious and socially responsible. I don't think it is a particular product or service. More important is your attitude and your commitment to fulfilling the social goal." Eventually, Kim's Save a Tree business picked up momentum and was mentioned in the popular book *50 Simple Things You Can Do to Save the Earth.* The business is now run by a family member, and the canvas bag concept has inspired other bags, and other markets.

Kim Marienthal's comments regarding social commitment ring particularly true in Anita Roddick's case. Roddick founded the Body Shop, a cosmetics retailing empire that has become as famous for its principles — such as no product testing on animals — as it has for the products it sells. In her book *Body and Soul,*

Roddick writes, "How do you ennoble the spirit when you are selling something as inconsequential as a cosmetic cream? You do it by creating a sense of holism, of spiritual development, of feeling connected to the workplace, the environment, and relationships with one another."

Returning soul to the workplace and making jobs more meaningful often boils down to not just what people do for a living but how they do it. Lawyers, for example, can use their skills to intimidate and antagonize, or to pursue justice through a healing hand and voice. A nonprofit educational organization called the International Alliance of Holistic Lawyers has formed with the precise intention of putting the heart back into the practice of law. This alliance, which is headquartered in Vermont, was founded by attorney Bill van Zyverden to offer an alternative approach to the type of hostile tactics that have given the legal profession such a bad image. Van Zyverden compares holistic law with holistic medicine. He says holistic lawyers are also engaged in healing; they try to settle issues through mediation and other techniques that leave people whole rather than torn apart.

The International Alliance of Holistic Lawyers offers workshops for members and the general public on how to resolve conflicts and disputes, and they eventually hope to change the curriculum in law schools so there is more emphasis on compassion and service to humanity.

WHOLE WORK

Holistic law. Holistic medicine. Business with soul. Teachers who address the whole student. Wherever one looks, professions are earnestly trying to embrace the better aspects of the human experience. When Kevin Sweeney at Patagonia described the need for quality products, he noted, "We have a holistic view. We understand the link between quality products and quality customer service, quality of life for employees, and quality of life on this earth. If the approach is piecemeal, the system falls apart because the commitment is not whole."

The character of work is carefully being reshaped. Rough and ugly edges still exist, but an earnest effort is under way to rebuild the workplace so it has more dignity and humaneness. When asked how business attitudes have changed during the last few years, especially in regard to environmental problems, Rebecca Calahan Klein, vice president of the Business for Social Responsibility Education Fund, replies, "I think a lot of companies have made the shift from thinking about environmental compliance as something they have to do because of regulations, to accepting that good environmental practices are integral to good business practices."

The best business practices radiate throughout society. More corporations are spending money on self-development courses for employees, fostering personal as well as professional growth. It is the corporation that is now aggressively promoting health maintenance, offering workshops on stress reduction and even meditation. It is the corporation that understands the strength of teamwork, creativity, and inner vision.

The institution of business, by its very adaptive nature, has the ability to ride risky roller coasters, alter its rules and mission, and change the course of our lives. The concept of people working in jobs that serve a positive purpose and the goal of uniting personal and professional lives so individuals can follow a synchronized route to self-fulfillment appear to be utopian wishes. Working to enrich the soul and benefit the planet may not yet be the norm in society, but they have become normal enough goals to turn the tide in the right direction. If we can create a whole new way of working, business can help us build nothing short of a whole new way of life.

CHAPTER FIVE

Whole Ways to Learn

The setting is a traditional classroom of fifth graders. It is near lunchtime and the students fidget as they watch their teacher write one more math problem on the blackboard. Above the blackboard a large sign outlines these class rules:

1. Be quiet.
2. Remain in seat unless given permission by teacher to leave.
3. Keep your desk neat and clean.

Besides a brief recess break, these children have been sitting at desks all morning, seldom talking except to answer the teacher's questions, or to sneak a quick word with a friend when the teacher isn't looking. As the teacher delivers further instructions, one child places a pencil between his teeth, and starts snapping his mouth up and down on it. Another taps his fingers on his desk in a steady, annoying beat. The girl beside him is concentrating on weaving her hair in and out of her fingers. At the back of the room a child giggles, but her smile quickly fades when the teacher looks in her direction.

Over the centuries, techniques for offering academic instruction have deviated little. Teachers present chalk-and-talk monologues, and students continue to write and recite like parrots. Learning remains depressingly shallow, as minds congeal in a cement of facts. Details are memorized in order to pass tests, but full understanding is not always achieved. If students become bored, inattentive, or outright nuisances in class, it is considered their fault, their problem.

But it has become everyone's problem. Isaac Fulwood, former police chief of Washington, D.C., now uses his free time to lecture on the connection between crime and education. "Eighty percent of the people we arrested were unemployed," he tells people. "They read at a 4.9 grade level. Their math skills were only at 3.5. They are going to jail because they have no ability to compete. Education is the key to freedom. Education gives people the ability to be free and make choices."

With too many teenagers dropping out of school, and countless others graduating without the skills required for gainful employment, the educational system faces a critical juncture. Many school reforms have been proposed, but most of these proposals are "more" or "less" solutions: more money, more parent involvement, fewer students in each class.

The restructuring of schools, however, is not just about changing the way we teach students. Schools are also redefining their purpose. One aim of education is to foster the growth of individual ability in whatever constructive form it takes. Yet to become a great human being is different from simply becoming great in a particular discipline. Our world is filled with people who have acquired considerable knowledge in a specialized area but use this knowledge unwisely because they haven't developed compassion or a conscience.

Most people agree that the key to solving societal problems lies in education, but this question remains: Is it schools' responsibility to teach students morality and ethics so they ultimately contribute to this world rather than harm it? Academic courses now prepare students for the job market, but should education also prepare students for life?

Many teachers fear criticism from community members and religious groups for influencing a student's social and moral development. But other teachers are discovering that as they change their teaching methods, it is relatively simple to highlight ethics, compassion, and the best human qualities in a way that avoids religion and makes sense to practically everyone. Linda Campbell, chair of teacher education at Antioch University in Seattle, points out that in the traditional competitive classroom, students are pitted against each other. Grades may improve but care for others suffers. Today, says Campbell, schools are moving toward collaborative ways of teaching and learning. This gives students opportunities to get to know each other, and acknowledge both differences and commonalities while working together to achieve shared goals. In such classrooms caring develops naturally.

"With basic research as a powerful ally," she says, "we are learning how to cultivate the vast potential of all people at every age and every ability level. The unfettering of potential at all levels of education comes at a time when global issues demand a new purpose of education. Our new goal can be no less than to nurture the compassionate genius within each of us."

Our educational system is being forced to change because it is languishing, but Campbell's point that "research is a powerful ally" provides a far more positive impetus for transformation. Recent scientific research has revealed new information about how humans learn and how we develop socially. In the past, schools have been inundated with trendy new teaching methods, and in their effort to avoid falling victim to new fads, administrators are inclined to be overly cautious. Even so, the new research on learning styles and how the human mind operates is so compelling that many schools are changing teaching techniques. Their success stories can inspire others to follow suit.

A MATTER OF STYLE

Before teachers can begin to address the three Cs (conscience, compassion, character) they first have to teach the traditional three Rs. If you point to the academic success of any exemplary school, skeptics will immediately counter with the challenge: What about troubled students, or students who just have trouble learning anything? Dr. Thomas Armstrong is a psychologist and educational consultant who has spent several years in public and parochial schools tending to children with learning problems. He contends that millions of students are falsely branded as learning disabled. "It became clear to me," he says, "that schools don't pay enough attention to each child's innate abilities."

In particular, the majority of schools still don't address different learning styles, he says, even though information about learning styles has been available to educators for well over a decade. The best-known researcher in this field is Dr. Rita Dunn, director of the Center for Study of Learning and Teaching Styles at St. John's University in New York City. Dunn holds the same opinion as Armstrong about learning disabilities. "Children are not learning disabled," she says vehemently. "They are *teaching* disabled. Maybe 80 percent of underachievers are global, tactile, kinesthetic children who can learn anything when taught correctly. Restructuring schools will not change anything unless they begin to deal with how each person learns."

Rita Dunn and her partner Kenneth Dunn have unequivocally demonstrated that such factors as time of day, sound, light, and whether youngsters work best by themselves, in pairs, or as a team, all affect how a student learns. Some individuals remember information when they hear it; others need visual aids or experiential activities.

When teaching methods accommodate different learning styles, the results can be dramatic, as illustrated in the following story. Several years ago, Bart Kelleher of the Buffalo, New York, school district had the responsibility of finding ways to help students who deviated from the norm. His desk was stacked with documentation about students with moderate to severe mental disabilities. These underachievers totaled 7,000 students from seventy-three schools in the Buffalo district.

In his search for solutions, Kelleher talked to one teacher who had participated in the Dunn and Dunn learning-style training program, who claimed it was a quick way to improve a student's performance. So Kelleher decided to take the training program himself. After the program, he agreed the concept had merit and persuaded Buffalo's Special Education Department to conduct their own research project on learning styles. Volunteer students were split into two groups; one group was taught the learning styles method, while the other students acted as a control group. Each student in the experimental group was matched with a student in the comparison group of the same age, disability, gender, and ethnicity.

On the first day, remembers Kelleher, the teachers complained it was impossible to run a classroom where each child pursued a different learning style. "I told them, give me six weeks, and if you want to quit you can," he says. "No one has ever quit."

After one year in the study, the experimental students showed significant improvement in math and reading skills compared to the control group. Today, over 100 teachers use the learning styles approach in the Buffalo district, and they are planning to train even more teachers. Special education in Buffalo, says Kelleher, has undergone its own revolution.

When describing an effective teaching method, people usually dwell on test results, but Kelleher, formerly a school counselor, knows how important it is to raise the human spirit, along with exam scores. He delights in telling these stories: "One student who had been diagnosed as mentally retarded said to me, 'I never knew I was so smart.' Another youngster, who had a severe mental disability, became curious about the bones in the body. The teacher gave him the time to explore information on the computer. He was a tactile, physically active learner and so the computer was an ideal vehicle for him. On his own he learned the names of most of the bones, and one day his teacher told him, 'You know more than I do.' It stopped the student in his tracks. He said, 'How can I know more than you?' The teacher replied, 'I'm only the coach here.'"

When teachers work in a learning-styles classroom, observes Kelleher, they become the coplanner with the student. It is the student who reveals to the teacher his or her preferred style of operating. "From a motivational point of view," he says, "you are finally saying to a kid, tell me about you, tell me what you do best and how you learn, and we will plan from there. I am not going to take the curriculum and impose it upon you. A number of youngsters can remember what they read if they walk. Well simple. Let them walk. It is their classroom. We don't need to have everybody at a desk. We need to have everybody actively learning. We're empowering students to know how to have initiative, how to be responsible, and respect differences. Ultimately, we return a lot of dignity to the child who has been told he is not measuring up."

THE WHOLE SCHOOL APPROACH FOR "AT-RISK" STUDENTS

Poverty, cultural differences, or linguistic barriers can also limit educational progress. Henry M. Levin, a Stanford University professor of education, considers it essential to also return dignity to these children. Traditionally, most of these students have been placed in remedial rote-training classes where they are expected to keep working at the same low-level skills until they have mastered them, but they often get further and further behind, and many finally drop out of school. The price they pay, and society pays, for this loss is high.

To counter this cycle, Levin founded the Accelerated Schools Project, based on the principle that teachers need to treat so-called "at-risk" students the same way they treat gifted students — empower them, don't restrict them. To empower children, says Levin, teachers shouldn't focus on academic weaknesses, but instead build on existing strengths and thus accelerate learning.

The Accelerated Schools movement has spread to over 1,000 elementary and middle schools throughout the United States. When conventional schools with high concentrations of disadvantaged students convert to an accelerated school, one of the first tasks is building a unanimous school spirit — not an easy task at what are often the worst schools in the district, known as "dumping grounds" for at-risk kids. What these students need most of all is emotional, as well as practical, support. They require the kind of commitment and extra effort that can only be offered from the heart. Therefore, the school asks for — and uses — everybody's help. By working together, teachers, students, parents, and community members begin by developing a vision of a school where all children can succeed.

What makes the Accelerated Schools Project different is that the entire school becomes involved in this transformational journey. Although individual teachers in individual classrooms have experienced success after adopting innovative teaching methods, this success can be magnified if every staff member is trained in these teaching techniques. The goal is school-wide change, with an emphasis on a whole-systems approach.

For instance, teachers try to make lessons relevant to the learner, helping students relate what they are experiencing in the classroom to real situations. In one fourth grade classroom, friends of a student with diabetes asked their math teacher why the student needed so many shots. The teacher could have answered the question simply, but seeing their curiosity about the human body she invited the school nurse to talk to the class. Bringing a skeleton with her, the nurse explained how the leg bone is called a "fibula" — leading to a discussion about Latin and its influence on the development of the English language. Using an integrated approach, the teacher also showed how math was pertinent to this topic. She arranged for the children to visit a local hospital, where a doctor talked about diabetes and its impact on human blood. Following the visit to the blood lab, the students learned how to do the necessary calculations to read blood test results. They took one another's pulse and calculated their blood pressure, discovering ratios and fractions in the process. The lesson on Latin roots of medical terms eventually turned into a history and language arts project.

By visiting the hospital, this teacher followed an Accelerated School model: to work collaboratively with community members. Collaboration is particularly important in building productive relationships with parents. In the past, many parents have been conspicuously absent from school activities. But when the teachers call personally and invite parents to participate in hands-on activities in the classroom, and have a say about what happens in their child's education, they begin to realize how much their contributions are valued. At Miami East North Elementary School in Ohio, parent volunteer hours went from 198 to over 2,000.

This collaborative whole-school-community atmosphere has also substantially increased attendance at parent-teacher conferences. In many accelerated schools parents can take part in programs that advance their own learning skills, which in turn prepares them to help their children.

Although some progress can be seen immediately, it takes several years to transform a school fully. This is why Levin talks about the Accelerated School Project not as a set plan but a flexible process — one that invites reflection and willingness to work together in the long-term to solve problems and reinforce positive expectations. To aid this process, each school has a coach — someone who can guide, prod, and encourage others. The coach soothes the way through obstacles and provides indispensable ongoing support. Eventually, test scores begin to rise and disciplinary problems decline.

A QUESTION OF VALUES

Despite such progress, educators throughout the nation are facing an uphill struggle as behavioral problems, from vandalism to violence, become commonplace. The Josephson Institute's 1996 Report Card on American Integrity showed a disturbing number of young people who are willing to lie, cheat, and steal. Their survey of more than 8,000 American high school and college students found that 42 percent of high school males, and 31 percent of high school females, had stolen something from a store within the previous twelve months. Sixty-five percent of high school students admitted they had recently cheated on an exam. One-third of college students also said they had cheated, and one-quarter of college students acknowledged they would lie to get or keep a job. As for violence in high schools, more than half the males and one-third of females said it is sometimes justified to respond to an insult or verbal abuse with physical force.

This survey also included about 3,000 adults. Forty percent of them said they would (or probably would) lie about a child's age to save money at an amusement park. However, among college students, a higher figure — 71 percent — said they would lie to save a few dollars.

According to such figures, the ethics of America's youth appear worse than the ethics of older generations. Before we rush to judge this generation, however, the Josephson Institute offers this perspective: They stress that today's youngsters are not "moral mutants" but rather that "the operational ethics of many young people is simply an amplified echo of the worst aspect of the adult world."

Nevertheless, they note that "the hole in moral ozone is getting bigger." As stated at the beginning of this chapter, the issue of whether schools should be directly involved in students' social and moral development is highly controversial. In most schools, social and moral maturation is an afterthought, or an after-school responsibility delegated to parents. In an ideal world, we could leave the shaping of a child's character to the family, community, and the neighborhood church. Unfortunately, with both parents working, a high divorce rate, and the breakdown of extended families and community, many parents feel overwhelmed; sometimes their fragmented lifestyles become part of the problem, not part of the solution.

So what is the solution? Sanford McDonnell, chairman emeritus of McDonnell Douglas Corporation, offers, "The more I think about it, the more I realize that intellectual knowledge without good character is actually dangerous. President Teddy Roosevelt said, 'To educate a man in mind, and not in morals, is to educate a menace to society.'" As head of a large corporation, McDonnell has been directly involved in promoting ethical business practices. Several years ago he developed a code of conduct for his employees, but he didn't stop there. He has also worked with schools to help them fund and establish character education programs, and specifically formed an effective school-business-community partnership that promotes a program called the "Personal Responsibility Education Process (PREP)."

In St. Louis, Missouri, more than thirty school districts have become involved with PREP, developing an explicit values-oriented school curriculum that has the support of parents and teachers. One of the reasons why PREP has been so successful is that it has dealt straightforwardly with the thorny issue of "whose values are going to be taught?" PREP encourages both parents and teachers in each school to decide the specific values and character traits they want to develop. If everybody doesn't agree on a value, then they don't use it.

This simple process illustrates how easily people from different backgrounds can come to a consensus about the core values they consider essential — values such as honesty, responsibility, respect, cooperation, and service to others. Each school also decides how they want to teach these values. At the Wedgwood Elementary School in St. Louis, for example, teachers focus on one character trait every month, and deliberately interweave the lessons into the daily curriculum. If a teacher is reading a story that mentions someone helping someone else, then the class stops and talks about it; if a student acts responsibly, then he or she is congratulated. Values become words and actions that are reinforced over and over again until they are integrated into the school's language and the whole environment.

Of course, there have always been teachers who have tried to go beyond facts to address matters of human character, but the difference between an individual's attempts and the concerted effort of an entire school faculty is dramatic. Jo Ann Jasin, the former principal of Wedgwood and executive director for curriculum of the Fergusen Florissant school district, remarks, "When a whole community bands together and says these values are important for all human beings, no matter what race, color, creed, or religion, it legitimizes the effort. All the education in the world is for naught, if we do not have kind, compassionate people coming out of our schools, who have a sense of right and wrong, who have respect for themselves and others, who know what it is to have a work ethic, and who are responsible for their own behavior."

Responding to the concern that only parents should instill "family values," Barbara Wright, the principal at Commons Lane School in St. Louis, takes this stance: "We realize parents can't do it all. *We* can't do it all. That is why we emphasize that we are all working together for the good of your child."

The PREP program in St. Louis is only one of many programs throughout the United States that promote character education. (To find out about other organizations, see this book's Resource Guide.) The Center for the Advancement of Ethics and Character, founded in 1989, was the first organized group in the country to specifically help teachers and administrators handle ethical and character issues in the classroom. They have recently written a one-page character education manifesto, which concludes, "Character education is not merely an educational trend or the school's latest fad; it is a fundamental dimension of good teaching, an abiding respect for the intellect and spirit of the individual. We need to reengage the hearts, minds, and hands of our children in forming their own characters, helping them 'to know the good, love the good, and do the good.'" This manifesto has been signed by over forty renowned educators and several governors.

THINKING ABOUT THINKING

With our children facing increasingly complex problems in society, educators agree on one other point: It is crucial to develop in students the ability to think critically and creatively. At an educational conference for teachers, Dr. Arthur Costa, emeritus professor at California State University, Sacramento, related a personal story to demonstrate to other teachers why we must avoid smug assumptions about how a student becomes a skillful thinker. Costa told the audience about buying a new garage door opener and trying to install it. He took it out of the box, spread the bits and pieces over the garage floor, and spent all morning attempting to follow the instructions. Around lunchtime, Kenney, his handyman, arrived at his house. Costa had previously arranged for Kenney to work on another household task, but when he saw him, he immediately asked for his help with the garage door opener.

"It was very interesting to see what Kenney did," recalled Costa. "Kenney surveyed all this stuff, went over and picked up a piece, examined it, put it back down, and then with one grand gesture, bent down again and put the whole thing together perfectly. I said, 'Kenney how could you do that? I've been struggling with this thing all morning and you didn't even read the instructions.' He looked kind of sheepish and said, 'You know, Art, I only went through third grade. I never did learn how to read, but when you don't read you've got to think.'"

Costa also underscores another aspect of thinking. To many people, he says, learning how to think critically is an intellectual endeavor, with little to do with emotions or feelings. He maintains, however, that thinking is directly linked to good listening and a capacity to empathize with others. "One of the highest forms of mental ability is empathy," declares Costa. "Behaving empathically requires overcoming one's own egocentricity, detecting another's subtle emotional and physical cues, and perceiving a situation from another's point of view — a complex set of cognitive processes."

TAKING CARE TO TEACH CARE

In many respects, the health of a democratic society revolves around empathy. Educated citizens are the backbone of a democracy, but in the long run a democracy can only prosper if these same citizens show the capacity to connect with others — to care about the welfare of all people, not just themselves.

One program that demonstrates how to promote caring in the classroom curriculum is the Child Development Project, which was first introduced in California and has now spread to several states — another program that hopes to achieve academic and character education simultaneously.

The Child Development Project uses the best available research on childrens' social development, but most of its techniques are surprisingly simple. In CDP schools, teachers avoid manipulating a child's behavior through external rewards or punishments. Instead, they explicitly help the children understand the reasons for rules and, when appropriate, even ask students for ideas about how to handle problems. While this may sound idealistic, it works for the most part because the children begin to feel part of a school community where trust is valued.

By weaving the program into a normal classroom day, consideration of other people becomes routine behavior. Teachers promote self-control and concern for others through cooperative learning sessions. Although many schools now structure classes so that children work together in small groups, cooperative learning can be a disappointment if students aren't given the skills to interact harmoniously with each other. At CDP schools, students are specifically taught how to work in groups. The goal is to teach them how to contribute positively to any social group, at any time in life.

Older students are also paired with younger students from other grades so that as "buddies" they can periodically help one another. In addition, teachers encourage the children to participate in acts that benefit the outside community.

"We use the term 'broadening the boundaries of caring,'" says Eric Schaps, CDP's director. "Each child learns to care not just about his or her own family members, or the school community, or the surrounding community, but eventually develops this notion that caring can be global."

Another way of encouraging students to care about others is to kindle interest in public service. As mentioned in chapter 2, many schools and colleges now have internal public service programs. Brooke Beaird is the associate director of National Campus Compact, an organization that develops volunteering opportunities on college campuses. Each year, over 800,000 students at Campus Compact member schools across the nation spend about 28 million hours of service in their communities. Beaird has observed that when students donate their time and talent, they gain exposure to experiences that help them cross the bridge between book-based idealism and purposeful action.

They also find volunteering is a two-way street. "The surprising part of volunteer work is how it cuts into the soul of the student who does the work," Beaird says, describing what happens when college students act as mentors to at-risk middle school students. "The at-risk youth obviously is in great need of the support of a caring adult, but the college students also become attached to the youngsters they're matched with and invariably they're overwhelmed with how much they get out of the relationship. There is a tendency to think of oneself as the white knight charging in to save someone. These students cease to see themselves as the white knight, and instead see themselves as a partner in a relationship that is very real and warm."

THE NEW VIEW OF INTELLIGENCE

Teaching students how to care for one another, or encouraging students to volunteer, places emotions center stage. Recently, thanks to the bestselling book *Emotional Intelligence* by psychologist and science writer Daniel Goleman, we are acknowledging the importance of teaching students how to understand and manage their emotions. As Goleman writes, a person with a high IQ can be emotionally illiterate. The consequences of emotional illiteracy, he says, can be tragic, from a personal as well as societal perspective. Such social problems as child abuse and even murder are commonly sparked by a lack of emotional self-control.

The concept of a distinct emotional intelligence has major implications. Indeed, due to research by Harvard psychologist Howard Gardner, we know there is a whole range of different intelligences. Within the last few years, the definition of "intelligence" has completely changed, and this reappraisal more than anything else is now reshaping what is being taught and how it is taught.

Schools too often treat students as if they were identical, squeezing them into a single teaching mold. Our modern educational system was designed to focus on linguistic and logical-mathematical abilities; if students display weakness in these areas, their intelligence is often questioned. In 1983, however, Gardner outlined in his book *Frames of Mind* at least seven different forms of intelligence. These intelligences, he said, operate in relative independence from each other, although people usually exhibit a blend of competencies, with varying degrees of strength in each area. His findings offered a far more expansive view of human potential than scientists and laypersons had ever considered. Along with linguistic and logical-mathematical abilities, Gardner listed spatial, musical, bodily-kinesthetic, and social intelligences, labeled "interpersonal" and "intrapersonal." (Before Gardner, the last five intelligences had been viewed as side talents, not part of the scope of human intellect.)

Gardner's research attracted a great deal of publicity, but his final conclusion is often overlooked. He warns that if a culture doesn't value a specific intelligence, and doesn't aggressively encourage its development, skills can remain undetected and undeveloped. Without question, the most undeveloped skills in our Western culture are the social intelligences — intrapersonal intelligence being the ability to cultivate insight into oneself, and interpersonal intelligence, the gift of understanding others. It is these intelligences that forge great leaders, compassionate health professionals, and skilled teachers and parents. Although we applaud such skills, we haven't as a society actively nurtured them. Yet, if we are to resolve urgent societal problems, our survival depends not just on how clever we can become technologically, but on how we solve conflicts and make judgments based on understanding ourselves and one another.

Recently, Gardner has provided evidence for an eighth intelligence called "naturalist intelligence." A naturalist, he explains, is an individual, such as John James Audubon, Rachel Carson, or Charles Darwin, with an extraordinary knowledge of the living world. In everyday life, we find farmers, gardeners, and others who clearly care about the environment all draw on this intelligence. In an era when our environment is reaching a crisis point, an understanding of this ability couldn't come at a better time.

Gardner has always said that other intelligences could be discovered. He is investigating the possibility of an existential intelligence — a concern with "ultimate" issues — and he even speculates that a spiritual intelligence might exist. "I would assume," he says, "that a spiritual intelligence would be especially attuned to those human needs of connectedness to a larger realm — human and natural — coupled with the ability to help oneself and/or others effect that connection."

A distinct spiritual or existential intelligence, however, is still highly speculative, and Gardner admits that these specialized areas demand far more careful analysis.

THE KEY TO ALL THE INTELLIGENCES

In the meantime, several schools have demonstrated how relatively easy it is to address the different intelligences. The Key Learning Community in Indianapolis, for example, was the first public school in the United States to put Gardner's theory of multiple intelligences into practice. Eight teachers initiated the bold school reform venture, persuaded the school district and the teachers' union to back their ideas, and finally started their own public elementary school. This school proved so successful that a middle school was also established.

At the elementary level, teachers determine at an early age if a child has a particular strength in one of the intelligences. Rather than relying on tests, the school initiated an unusual approach: Teachers watch how children play games. Based on creativity and motivation research by Mihaly Csikszentmihalyi, an author and professor of psychology at the University of Chicago, the teachers designed what they call a "Flow Activity Center," set up with a wide variety of games that represent the seven intelligences. The staff observes which activities the children prefer and how the students interact with one another. Over time the teachers can detect each student's intrinsic interests and whether he or she excels in a certain area. The idea is to then bolster natural talents, and both the elementary and middle school allot special times in the week for students to work with teachers and outside specialists in the community who can help develop individual skills.

The different intelligences are also consciously interwoven throughout the curriculum. For instance, spatial intelligence is accentuated in geography, while social intelligences fall naturally under history. To these teachers, history is more than dates, wars, and revolutions; it is the story of interpersonal relationships, and due to the curriculum's interdisciplinary style, such subjects are treated with greater depth.

Grade levels are also mixed at the Key schools. While in traditional single grade classrooms, top students usually remain at the top, one advantage of multiage grouping, say these teachers, is that students discover what it is like to work their way up the ladder of knowledge. Initially they are the novice, then the middle person, and then in the third year they become the experts in the class. The teachers feel this process also develops the social intelligences, because the students become adept at interacting with all types of people and through group activities come to understand how everyone has something to contribute.

THE ULTIMATE LESSON

People often say, "children are our future." This phrase returns the awesome responsibility of putting into practice today what we would like to see happen tomorrow. Dee Dickinson is the director of New Horizons for Learning, a global human resource network dedicated to improving education. "Never in the history of the world," she reflects, "has it been more essential to reinvent our educational systems. The need for well-educated, ethical, and empathetic members of every society grows in direct proportion to the increasing apathy, poverty, and violence in our communities."

With the internet, she adds, the educational process has become even more complex. Rapidly changing information on every conceivable subject — fact and fiction — is now available. "Educational systems must not only help students learn basic skills, and gain basic knowledge," cautions Dickinson, "but of even greater importance, they must help students learn how to access information and determine what is useful and accurate."

What concerns Dickinson the most is that too many teachers and parents still equate education with a quiet, passive classroom. "It is crucial teachers respect and honor each person as a unique human being with different learning styles and strengths," she says. "This can only be done in classrooms where students' individual needs are recognized, where they have opportunities to engage in thoughtful dialogue, and opportunities to apply what they have learned in meaningful contexts."

The latest information on how the brain functions is confirming that when teachers pay more attention to the whole person, learning improves. The brain functions optimally, claim researchers, when tasks are intrinsically interesting, and when the mind, body, and senses are involved. This means students have to become active participants, rather than passive learners. Sound, touch, movement, and feelings all must be ignited — with the emphasis on feelings; if the heart isn't involved, the head won't be either.

Although many schools are changing the way they educate students, replicating their success throughout the nation's school system will be a challenge. "It will take a major commitment of time and money," says Dickinson, "to assure that professors of education, and all teachers of students, start utilizing current information on how we can elicit the fullest possible development of each individual."

What is most exciting in education today is that we have only just begun to comprehend the richness of our potential — especially the lessons of the heart and spirit.

CHAPTER SIX

The Environmental Connection

Environmentalists are often criticized for being more concerned about trees and animals than human welfare. We pit predicaments against one another, such as loss of jobs versus loss of natural resources. Yet, as Paul Downton, president of Urban Ecology Australia, once quipped, "No ecology — no economy; no planet — no profits."

During the last two decades, as we have addressed serious environmental concerns, we have learned a great deal about connections between issues. Author and physicist Fritjof Capra was one of the first individuals to speak up about the need for a whole systems approach to preserving our planet. Capra is the founder of the Center for Ecoliteracy, an organization that helps educators and students understand and practice the principles of ecology. Through his books and lectures, he has been emphasizing one single point: "It is crucial to recognize that the major problems of our time are all systemic problems, which means that they are all interconnected and interdependent. None of them can be understood in isolation."

Understanding the interconnections of the world's problems is only half the story. The most hopeful part of the message that Capra and others are trying to deliver is that just as problems are intertwined, so are the solutions.

"In fact," writes Capra, "the more we study the situation, the more we realize that all these problems — environmental degradation, poverty and hunger, the threat of nuclear war, population growth, whatever problems you take — are just different facets of one single crisis, which is largely a crisis of perception. Only if we perceive the world differently will we be able to act differently. So we need a change of perception, a shift of paradigms in our thinking and in our values. We need a shift from fragmentation to wholeness, from a mechanistic view of the world to an ecological view, from domination to partnership, from quantity to quality, from expansion to conservation, from efficiency to sustainability."

This call for a complete shift in the way we perceive the world isn't new. Throughout human history, we have been continuously asked — or forced — to change our perceptions of life. Americans used to think slavery was normal. We also thought it normal for women not to vote. The evolution of the human species has been marked by many mind-changing milestones. But the environmental threat is more than just another wake-up call to change our habits. Experts are telling us that if we don't strive for a higher standard of human conduct toward each other and the environment, we run the risk of bringing about the end of our existence on this planet.

Each year the Worldwatch Institute, a nonprofit research organization, publishes a State of the World Report assessing the gains and losses of natural resources. This report is distributed to the world's leaders in hopes of influencing world politics. Along with sounding the alarm about impending devastation, it outlines the policy measures required to construct a sustainable environment and a sound economy.

"We know what we have to do. And we know how to do it," writes Lester Brown, president and senior researcher of the Worldwatch Institute. But, he warns, "If we fail to convert our self-destructing economy into one that is environmentally sustainable, future generations will be overwhelmed by environmental degradation and social disintegration."

This grim prognosis was first forecast in the 1970s. At that time, a special computer model was used by a team of scientists from the Massachusetts Institute of Technology to investigate the long-term consequences of economic growth. The scientists concluded that if the growth trends continued, the earth would reach its limits within the next one hundred years. These predictions of possible doom, published in a book called *The Limits to Growth,* created a furor. Millions of copies of the book were sold around the world, evoking a vigorous debate about the results of the computer's predictions.

Now, in the '90s, the scientists have updated their original findings, this time using a computer model to integrate statistical information with scientific and economic theory about the global system. The results are even more devastating. They found that the world has already gone beyond its limits in some areas, and the likelihood of a global economic collapse is closer than ever.

However, the scientists are not delivering, and have never intended to deliver, an apocalyptic vision. Biophysicist Donella Meadows, one of the authors of *The Limits to Growth,* who was involved in both computer studies, emphasizes it is still possible to correct these problems. Even so, she tells a revealing story of what occurs when she and her Norwegian colleague and coauthor Jørgen Randers appear together before an audience.

"Twenty years ago, when our first book was published," she says, "Jørgen thought that once we told the world about the problems, the world would turn on a dime and start going in a different direction. Today he presents the new findings with total cynicism. He tells the audience, 'Nobody is going to pay any attention. Forget it. It's over. We're going to collapse.' When he does that the entire audience rises to tell him, 'No! no! no! We can change things. There's time.'

"But when I join in and tell the audience that I think a sustainable future is the one that is going to happen, then the entire audience rises and says, 'Oh, you silly idealist. Here are all the reasons why that won't happen.'

"What I have come to see," continues Meadows, "is that there's no basis for being sappily hopeful, and there's no basis for being bitterly cynical. Each reaction is an oversimplification."

Audience cynicism peaks when Meadows begins to explain how we can achieve an equitable, sustainable world, because her solutions require more than technological or economic fixes. To stop environmental destruction, she says, and to prevent starvation and misery in the world, we will first have to undergo a human revolution — a revolution of the human heart. We won't solve our problems, contends Meadows, unless we foster genuine care for nature, along with genuine care for other human beings. Usually after each speech Meadows delivers, at least one person tells her, "If there is any scarce resource on this planet it is love."

What isn't scarce is pessimism. Meadows and her colleagues make this observation in their more recent book, *Beyond the Limits*: "The deepest difference between optimists and pessimists is their position in the debate about whether human beings are able to operate collectively from a basis of love. In a society that systematically develops in people their individualism, their competitiveness, and their cynicism, the pessimists are in the vast majority.

"That pessimism is the single greatest problem of the current social system, we think, and the deepest cause of unsustainability. A culture that cannot believe in, discuss, and develop the best human qualities is one that suffers from a tragic distortion of information."

They stress, "The sustainability revolution will have to be, above all, a societal transformation that permits the best of human nature rather than the worst to be expressed and nurtured."

THE INTERRELATEDNESS OF LIFE

In subtle ways, the sustainability revolution, because of its systemic thinking, has started to alter not only the way we look at the world, but how we act. To sense how the new scientific story of the cosmos is changing attitudes, consider some of the revisions taking place in the field of biology.

Biologist Brian Goodwin is a program coordinator for holistic science at Schumacher College in England. He is affiliated with an international group of biologists who are dissatisfied with the idea that you can explain life solely in terms of natural selection and the function of different mechanical parts. Fragmentation, they contend, delivers a distorted perspective, because when you reduce organisms to a collection of genes you see only a mechanical interpretation of life. Goodwin and the other biologists claim nature has a deep intelligibility; biology is driven by far more than function and utility. To understand this intelligibility, says Goodwin, you have to start with the whole organism and take into account how life forms not only interact with one another but work together. These biologists believe that the intrinsic order and unity of the living world cannot be explained by an evolution based on chance; organisms are not just passively influenced by natural selection or random genetic variation. In their view, organisms have the power of self-organization. The new biology depicts an organism as a dynamic form that is constantly changing. Evolution looks more like a creative dance — a continuous exploration of possibility.

By revising our concept of how life evolves, says Goodwin, we can also gain a grander view of how we, as humans, live and thrive on this planet. "What can a new biology contribute to a new consciousness and a new form of action in the world?" he asks. "Well, the new biology gives us a model of totality that is continually in the process of transformation. The organism, which is a reflection and an affirmation of this primal unity, then becomes a kind of metaphor through which we can understand process, transformation, cooperation, mutualism, and subtle forms of interaction that are positive and beneficial."

Because a biology of wholeness confirms the interrelatedness of life, we are being compelled, believes Goodwin, to alter self-centered behavior. "Because everything is connected you cannot take action in one place without affecting everything else," he says. "Therefore, every new action must be taken with great caution. It provides another value system — to have as much respect for the pebble on the beach as you do for yourself."

CONNECTING RELIGION WITH ENVIRONMENTAL ISSUES

On a practical level, the scientific recognition of the interrelatedness of life has made us more acutely sensitive to environmental issues, but it is on the personal level where we catch a glimpse of its spiritual effect.

Acknowledging the divine in the earth's creation is a natural connection for the religious, and hence the religious community is beginning to respond vigorously to the environmental crisis.

During 1991, a number of meetings took place between senior religious leaders and eminent scientists, including several Nobel Laureates. These scientists presented scientific documents detailing how the earth is being destroyed, often by human greed and short-sightedness. Then the scientists said something extraordinary. They told the religious leaders that in their view the environmental crisis was a spiritual as well as scientific challenge because of the ethical questions connected to these problems. They wanted, therefore, to work with the religious establishment to promote environmental activism.

It was the start of a formal coalition in which several religions found themselves breaking down divisions and working together to protect the planet. The National Religious Partnership for the Environment was created, an alliance of the U.S. Catholic Conference, the National Council of Churches of Christ, the Coalition on the Environment and Jewish Life, and the Evangelical Environmental Network. These groups have a combined membership of roughly 100 million people, and their efforts show what can happen when people unite to solve a crisis. As Paul Gorman, the executive director of this partnership, says, "The religious community has the ability to reach millions of people, and scientists don't."

The alliance continues to reach these millions through educational kits and programs that discuss how to preserve the environment and also how to see such actions as both a moral and spiritual responsibility.

"People understand, although they don't always live up to it that to be religious is to care for the poor and the destitute," says Gorman, "The churches have soup kitchens and programs for poor people. It is what you do out of your faith. In the same way, caring for creation has to become an intrinsic and fundamental part of what it means to be religious."

NATURAL STEPS TO SAVE THE ENVIRONMENT

Despite these positive developments, it is still difficult to get the majority of the world's population to pay more than lip service to environmental concerns. To complicate matters, scientists inevitably assess the severity of environmental threats very differently. And because immediate profits are continually valued more than the long-term preservation of natural resources, most business leaders are reluctant to change their ways. Finding common ground seems an impossible task.

Yet, with the right approach, it *is* possible. This story begins with one man, Karl-Henrik Robert, a leading cancer researcher in Sweden, who became frustrated at hearing the various arguments and counterarguments about what should and shouldn't be done to protect the environment. He felt there had to be a way to stop bickering and act. To Robert, it was like watching a house burn down while the fire brigade debated whether the fire was a big one or a small one, whether to put it out, and how to put it out.

He decided to see if more than fifty prominent scientists in Sweden could come to a consensus about environmental problems. Rather than arguing about peripheral details, could these scientists find common ground if they focused on fundamental concerns at the systemic level?

A consensus report was drafted and revised over twenty times before everyone agreed on all the facts. The King of Sweden even endorsed the report. But that was just the beginning. Robert arranged for millions of copies to be distributed to every Swedish household and school; Swedish TV agreed to help with an educational campaign, where famous artists and celebrities appeared on television to explain how the entire Swedish society could join in the effort to make their way of life healthier and more sustainable. After participating in dialogues about the report, Electrolux, the largest household appliance manufacturer in the world, agreed to find an alternative to CFCs in their refrigerators and freezers; they now use a compound that doesn't harm the ozone layer. Other businesses have also changed their manufacturing techniques. Throughout Sweden, study circles have been established so people can continue to discuss these issues and find ways to act.

Robert calls this collaborative process the Natural Step. It is the name of an organization, and also the name of the framework composed of scientifically based principles that serve as a compass to guide society toward environmental and socially responsible practices. The question remains whether other countries can replicate Sweden's outstanding success with this approach. Several countries are willing to try. The Natural Step has been introduced in the United States by Paul Hawken, who acts as chairman of the board of the American organization. Hawken is the visionary business leader who wrote *The Ecology of Commerce*, a book that examined the relationship between business and the environment.

During the last few years, as Hawken has traveled around the United States talking about how sustainability relates to commerce, he has noticed two developments. "One is that there is a huge drive toward sustainability," he says. "It is the fastest growing movement in the United States. But secondly, there is not a shared language regarding environmental concerns. Everyone perceives the problems slightly differently, or in some cases, vastly differently. Even when solutions exist to a given problem, those solutions are not adopted by society as a whole because society as a whole does not share the same definitions."

Yet Hawken found people could agree on the overall principles required for sustaining life on earth. The dialogue breaks down, he says, when individuals dwell on details and differences — all aggravated by personality clashes. Blame, criticism, and judgments — coupled with constant quibbling about a point here and a point there — are the stickiest hurdles to overcome. Hawken likens it to asking Republicans and Democrats to agree on certain passages in a piece of legislation. "They'll argue every step of the way," he observes. "But if you ask them what kind of world do they want to see their grandchildren living in, they will all come up with the same values — such as a safe, prosperous, clean environment, plus good health, and a good education."

To accomplish goals that are in everybody's self-interest, the Natural Step offers a training program to help businesses, government agencies, universities, and communities recognize and accept some fundamental conditions necessary for a sustainable life on earth — such as the fact that substances from the earth's crust, or substances produced by society, cannot systematically increase in the biosphere without harming our planet. When people are guided by a framework of scientifically based principles, says Hawken, it allows them to move from A to Z without getting stuck in the middle. And as individuals understand the core principles concerning ecological connections, based on nonnegotiable and indisputable scientific facts, then wise decisions about how to solve environmental problems naturally occur. Using the Natural Step process, people can eventually work, out of collective self-interest, toward a vision of the world we all desire.

FROM NATURE TO SOCIAL JUSTICE ISSUES

Few people link the environmental movement with social justice issues, but the connections are obvious if you talk to someone like Carl Anthony, a man who has devoted his life to two objectives: preserving the earth, and preserving the dignity of all individuals, regardless of race or economic position.

Anthony is acutely aware of the irony that diversity is glorified in nature but not always in humans. "How can you appreciate the diversity of species and the diversity of our biosphere, and then turn around and be unappreciative and totally blind to the diversity of the human race?" he says. "It is not an accident that these two forms of consciousness should emerge in the public discourse at almost exactly the same time."

Anthony is the director of the Urban Habitat Program, an environmental justice organization based in San Francisco. Trained as an architect, he uses his professional skills to revitalize run-down communities. His concern is that environmental problems have especially harmed poor people and people of color. Neighborhoods without political or economic power have become the dumping grounds for toxic waste and polluting industries. On a larger scale, the natural resources of poor countries have been ransacked by businesses seeking easy profits. And sometimes it is not just what we do, but what we don't do. A few years ago when thousands of Ethiopians were starving, it was not uncommon to hear that starvation was one way of controlling population. Anthony calls these actions and attitudes environmental racism.

He also weds environmental justice issues to a new field of study called ecopsychology. As the name suggests, this field examines how one's personal health is influenced by the health of the environment. For instance, says Anthony, many people of color, and those from the lower end of the economic ladder, have no choice but to live in the inner cities, where the environment is usually bleak and polluted. When you are surrounded by deterioration, and live in a polarized community, he continues, your emotional and physical health are readily affected.

This is the bad news, but Anthony is also gathering the good news. Through his magazine *Race, Poverty, and the Environment,* he is publicizing efforts to improve poor communities. Urban forests are being planted, and community gardens now flourish in the midst of housing projects. "The basic idea," he says, "is to amplify the voices in these communities, and create an atmosphere within the environmental movement that respects cultural diversity. The emerging environmental justice movement involves hundreds of grassroots organizations. In poor communities all around the country, people are saying, 'We want higher environmental standards, we don't want to be blackmailed, we don't want to be told we have to choose between having a job and having a clean environment.'"

One story Anthony enjoys telling is about an African-American woman named Cathrine Sneed who works as a counselor in a San Francisco jail. She wanted to give the prisoners a sense of self-worth and skills they could use when they left jail so she started a horticultural project on the prison land. She taught prisoners basic landscaping skills, and how to raise flowers, organic vegetables, and herbs. She also established a support program to employ former prisoners in growing produce.

Some of the organic vegetables the prisoners and ex-prisoners grow are given to seniors and the homeless, but the bulk is sold to farmers' markets and gourmet restaurants. When President Clinton visited San Francisco, one of the city's finest restaurants served him this produce. A contract has also been signed with the city of San Francisco, authorizing the former prisoners to plant street trees.

To Anthony, this story of renewal illustrates how the earth can soothe souls, while providing psychological and literal nourishment. As for Cathrine Sneed, she offers this opinion: "I truly believe that when people find themselves in jail, it is primarily because they have lost contact with themselves, their families, and their community. I think gardening and nature reconnects us. The beauty one can create through gardening empowers people. They look at what they have done in the garden and begin to pay attention to themselves, begin to feel as if they can make changes. When you take care of plants they flourish. What I try to do is help people see that just like plants flourish with care, people flourish with care."

A NEW VISION OF OUR TRUE NATURE

People commonly react to Cathrine Sneed's accomplishments with prisoners by calling her story an exception. It is difficult to accept that establishing links with nature can dramatically change a person's personality. In fact, many of us at least subconsciously view nature as cruel. The prevailing mythology that the natural world is ruled by violence and fierce competition can be partially traced to Darwin. Darwin's theory of natural selection (later coined, "survival of the fittest") was based on the premise that the main goal of animals and plants was reproduction, and that all of life centered around this struggle to reproduce and survive.

Yet scientific evidence gathered by philosopher Robert Augros and physicist George Stanciu indicates that nature uses ingenious techniques to elicit widespread cooperation. Augros and Stanciu assert that Darwin tried to understand nature by using Cartesian reductionism — the methodology of trying to understand the whole by studying isolated parts. "Then when he put all those isolated organisms back together, he thought it was clear that such reproduction would lead to a shortage of space, of food, and other necessities of life," Augros and Stanciu write. "There was going to be severe competition, and therefore all of nature was going to be at war."

Darwin's survival of the fittest concept has, to a great degree, been used to justify the self-serving every-person-out-for-himself-or-herself mentality. This cutthroat model of human nature was reinforced by the English philosopher Thomas Hobbes, who spearheaded the doctrine of individualism. Like Darwin, Hobbes also used reductionist techniques. He broke society down into isolated individuals and saw self-interest as the main drive behind human actions. To Hobbes there was no common purpose or common good, only individuals competing against other individuals for wealth and power. This political philosophy has seeped into our economic system and our entire Western way of life.

"We've paid a high price for this competitive mode," says Augros. "You can see it in the classroom, in sports, in the business world, but this is not the natural way for the human mind to operate. It is highly artificial and imposed on us by a cultural heritage that dates back to the nineteenth century."

Through their research, Augros and Stanciu show how cooperation and harmony are guiding principles in the natural world. To avoid competition, nature exhibits specific strategies, such as dividing the same habitat according to day and night shifts. Species also establish "territorial rights" to protect their home and food supply. Although nature films tend to dramatize territorial challenges between species, the purpose of establishing boundary lines or a pecking order is often to avoid conflict.

"Furthermore," says Augros, "it is not just a matter of avoiding violence and competition. There is a positive bent between species to help each other." He notes that when animals are incapable of cleaning their own bodies they receive aid from other species, and the benefits are often reciprocal. For example, the body of the hippopotamus is cleaned by labeo fish, but as it moves through the water it stirs up food for the fish and also churns up snails. When the hippopotamus surfaces, the storks catch a ride on its back hunting for these snails. The end result, he says, is a rich environment.

THE GOOD JANE GOODALL SEES

All the same, those who have researched the behavior of primates report that chimpanzees, which are said to be the human being's closest relative, are capable of aggressive and brutal behavior. Yet this fierce image has a flip side that has received too little attention. Dr. Jane Goodall, who is world renowned for her studies on chimpanzees at the Gombe National Park in Tanzania, states that chimpanzees also exhibit empathy and altruism. She tells the story of a sickly orphan, just over three years old, whose mother had died in an epidemic. Without an older brother or sister to adopt him, he followed one adult after another. "These adults, mostly males, were all nice to him," recalls Goodall, "but there was no special bond, which is what the young chimpanzee needs. However, he was eventually adopted by a twelve-year-old, nonrelated adolescent male. This adolescent male carried him, shared his food, slept with him, and rescued him from dangerous situations. We couldn't understand why a nonrelated adolescent male would burden himself with a sickly infant. What did he gain? Perhaps it helped fill a void in his life because the epidemic that claimed the infant's mother, killed his mother too. At any rate, he definitely saved the infant's life."

In 1996, a gorilla made the headlines when a three-year-old boy fell into a gorilla compound at a zoo in Illinois. The boy's life was saved by a female gorilla who cradled and stroked the child and then carefully left him by a door in the compound where he was rescued by zoo attendants.

Empathy, it seems, exists in the animal kingdom, and these signs of noble character speak well for human evolution. "We must understand," says Goodall, "that human tendencies toward compassion and altruism are very deeply inherited. We have found that chimpanzees, in particular, demonstrate both the good and the bad side of human nature."

After years of studying how primates behave, Goodall is interested in applying these lessons to human behavior. One of the main differences between humans and chimpanzees, she says, is that humans can understand the consequences of their actions. Therefore, through the Jane Goodall Institute for Wildlife Research, Education, and Conservation, she initiated a youth education program called Roots & Shoots to persuade young people that their actions can make a difference.

Roots & Shoots is a symbolic name: roots creep underground

to make a firm foundation; weak-seeming shoots can break through brick walls to reach the light. "We see the brick walls as all the problems humans have created on the planet, ranging from overpopulation, to soil erosion, desertification, famine, pollution, crime, and warfare," Goodall says. "The message is that thousands of roots and shoots around the world can break through, but this will only happen when each individual realizes he or she has a role to play. People have a choice whether they want to use their life to make the world around them a better or worse place."

Roots & Shoots began in 1991 in Tanzania, East Africa, and is now a worldwide program, offered mainly through schools and neighborhood groups. With the aid of constructive activities, Roots & Shoots teaches youngsters to show respect to all living things, and to care about their community by working on solutions to local problems. In Tanzania, youths plant trees. In the United States, the Los Angeles police department is piloting an inner-city program to change young attitudes and lives. The police arranged for children, some of whom had never seen the beach, to spend a day at the ocean learning about nature's beauty, and at the same time cleaning up beach litter.

An international youth network, Partnerships in Understanding, has also been established, so Roots & Shoots groups, whether they are in Tanzania or Tulsa, Oklahoma, can exchange program information. These young people from around the globe, says Goodall, are gradually gaining a better understanding of the interdependence of all life on earth. Ultimately she hopes they will be able to act together in a united effort to help resolve environmental and humanitarian challenges.

THE CARING CIRCLE

Just as we are inescapably vulnerable to destructive forces all over the globe, we also benefit any time anyone works to better humankind. Solutions and opinions vary about how to solve social and planetary problems, but the basic obligations of cooperation, decency, and concern for others remain constant. If anything, these obligations have become even more essential and urgent. In this interconnected world, information rapidly travels via computer to remote corners of the globe, and through television we can connect visually and emotionally with any country or any person making news. We have access to knowledge we have never had before, but attached to this knowledge are greater responsibilities — especially moral responsibilities.

Ten years ago, it was rare to hear a person raise the subject of love in a conversation about preserving the environment. Love may not be on everybody's lips, but a more hopeful message is beginning to emerge.

CHAPTER SEVEN

Living as a Work of Art

The arts are the open passageway to our hearts and souls, the direct route we can take to decipher the mysterious and ambiguous, and the direct means to express all that needs a voice and a vision. Yet we've had to plead for schools to include the arts in their curricula. We've also had to listen to others tell us that they aren't creative — can't paint, draw, write, play an instrument, carry a tune, can't even dance. Not only do too many of us deny our own creativity, many can't appreciate the creativity of others; they haven't been taught how to comprehend the subtleties and complexities of a story, poem, or painting. Worst of all, we don't mourn this loss.

Throughout these chapters, we've examined the divisions erected to separate different parts of our lives, the compartmentalization that has severed natural connections. As we explore the role of the arts in our society, the divisions appear almost impenetrable. In the United States, the arts have been shoved into such an inconsequential corner of our existence that many consider them nonessential — something that could, if necessary, be discarded. They are a thrill to some, a frill to others. In particular, the arts remain the orphans of our educational system, repeatedly left in a state of neglect and abandonment. Though the arts may have been a central influence in primitive cultures, and indeed most later civilizations, in our modern culture their importance is, amazingly enough, still a matter of debate. But if one thing is preventing us from living full lives, it is this missing part of ourselves.

STARRING ROLE IN SOCIETY

Whenever we as a society decide where to invest our time and money, it becomes painfully clear how little we value the arts. "The role of the arts in all communities is a matter of no less consequence that the role of science, health care, education, or defense," argues Michael Greene, president and CEO of the National Academy of Recording Arts and Sciences. "By refusing to invest in the arts, we are short-changing our communities and are in danger of developing culturally bankrupt societies."

Green says that the lack of monetary support for the arts does not stem from an unwilling American public. As a 1996 Louis Harris survey showed, not only do most Americans believe that the federal government should provide financial aid to arts programs but a majority of citizens are even willing to pay higher taxes to fund the arts. At present, it costs taxpayers less than fifty cents a year to finance the National Endowment for the Arts (NEA). Sixty-one percent of Americans would be willing to pay an additional $5 tax, and 56 percent said they would pay $10.

The same survey counted how many Americans attended art museums, the theater, or participated in the arts. The figure was 86 percent of the nation's adults — 165 million people. "These results put to rest decisively any claim that the arts are the province of the affluent and elite," says Harris. "Indeed, they are deeply rooted in the lives of the vast majority of the American people themselves. Significantly, 33 percent more of the American people participate in the arts than turn out to vote in a presidential election."

Since the NEA was founded in 1965, dance companies have increased from 37 to over 400, large symphony orchestras have doubled, and there are eight times as many theatrical companies. Sports fans might be surprised to know that the annual attendance for the performing arts now exceeds that for all professional sports combined.

So why do we consider the arts so inconsequential in our lives? Perhaps it's because although the pleasures of art are obvious, the arts have been pigeonholed for too long in the category of entertainment and decoration. We need to take another look at how *all* levels of our lives are affected. Could it be that the arts can teach us the fundamental truths of living?

One benefit is immeasurable: Music and art celebrate diversity; they heal cultural and political differences. "We have always heard," says Robert Commanday, a former music critic for the *San Francisco Chronicle,* "about music's universality, music as an international language bridging cultures, transcending differences. It's been said so often that no one notices when it really happens, or gives credit to the phenomenon."

Commanday, who once served on a U.S. State Department panel to help underwrite tours of artists to other countries, proposes it is time to give credit where it is due. "Music and dance," he reflects, "were the principal communication between the

Soviets and Americans for several decades of the Cold War, when normal contact was all but eliminated."

However, he also knows the difficulty of assessing the influence of the arts on our political consciousness. "The general response to art is ingenuous," he says. "It is a lot to expect an audience attending a concert of a foreign artist to think of the implications beyond the artistic experience. We may have to leave it up to the historians to analyze what kept the contact alive during the Cold War and what helped stave off more serious friction."

THE ART OF POLITICAL PERSUASION

For a story about art's gentle power of political persuasion, return to 1989, when Czechoslovakia was still in the grip of political repression. It was a time when police were cracking down on peaceful demonstrations; any independent political activity readily led to imprisonment. In this oppressive climate, singer Joan Baez visited the Czech city of Bratislava to give a concert.

The concert was sponsored by the Czechoslovakian government and was meant to be a straightforward performance, another stop in a European tour to celebrate the thirtieth anniversary of Joan Baez's singing career. When Baez arrived in the city, she invited a number of Czech human rights activists to be her guests. She also invited playwright Vaclav Havel, then known as a political dissident. To make sure Havel and the others weren't arrested on their way to the concert, Baez arranged to accompany her guests from her hotel to the concert site.

Traveling with Baez on this trip was Martha Henderson, who at that time was codirector of Baez's human rights organization, "Humanitas." When Havel arrived at the hotel, he told Henderson that he had been followed by five carloads of plainclothes police on his way to Baez's hotel. Fearful he still might be arrested, it was suggested that Havel sit next to Henderson during the concert. The idea was for Henderson to act as an international bodyguard to discourage the police from seizing him.

"Under such difficult circumstances," Henderson recalls, "small gestures have a big impact. Even something seemingly harmless, such as inviting people as guests to a concert becomes a controversial and visible action — and all the more important to do!"

When the concert began, Baez sang her most popular songs and also a favorite of the Polish solidarity leader Lech Walesa. When she mentioned his name the audience broke into spontaneous applause. She then dedicated another song to Charter 77, a civil rights manifesto introduced by Czechoslovakian intellectuals and workers seeking their government's compliance with the Helsinki Accord. At this point, the audience went wild while government officials, worrying about the songs' rousing effect, turned the microphones off.

But the authorities couldn't stop the concert, and afterwards they were unable to stop what has been called the nonviolent "velvet revolution," which led to Havel becoming the president of Czechoslovakia. Years later, in an interview with the American press, Havel reflected on this concert and credited Baez for arousing the consciousness of his people. "Our revolution had a number of steps that were in some way preparatory states," he observed. "One of these was, for example, the Joan Baez concert in Bratislava. She invited us there and spoke from the stage about Charter 77, and we agreed with many friends that the spirit of the '60s was somehow revived there with Baez, a symbol for the nonviolent '60s peace movement."

Artists have often awakened people to new political realities, and kept the flame of the human spirit alive during times of conflict and oppression. When the war in Bosnia was at its height, members of the Sarajevo Philharmonic Orchestra continued to rehearse and play while their city was under siege. Some of the musicians were injured by artillery fire, and they received a threat to level their concert hall if they didn't stop rehearsals. But they didn't stop. They weren't just playing music; they were playing to prevent the very essence of humanity and civility from being crushed.

Many artists also use their fame to raise money for political issues. In 1996, 100,000 music fans packed Golden Gate Park in San Francisco to listen to the Beastie Boys and other top rock and rap acts in a concert to promote a "Free Tibet." Bill Graham Presents produced the event, which raised more than $1 million for the Tibetan cause, while educating young listeners, who were willing to absorb the political message. But these concerts aren't just about money. Over a decade ago, American and Soviet rock bands played together at a free concert in Moscow produced by Bill Graham to honor antinuclear demonstrations. In 1989, when the Berlin Wall came down, a concert by and for the people was the choice of celebration, with Beethoven's Ninth Symphony passionately proclaiming the survival of the human spirit. In the pages of history we hear the politicians' voices, but many times it is the voice of the musician, artist, writer, and poet that endures.

PEACE THROUGH ART

The historic role of the arts in the peace process is documented in the Peace Museum, the first museum of its kind, located in Chicago. Stored within its walls are original manuscripts and artifacts by Joan Baez, Pete Seeger, Bono of the band U2, and other musicians who have worked for social change.

The Peace Museum exhibits also show how visual art can capture moments when words fail us. In their collection, for instance, are drawings by survivors of the atomic attacks on Nagaski and Hiroshima.

The museum doesn't just look back on history, but works for the future by seeking answers to present social issues, including domestic and street violence. Their antidote to drive-by shootings is a Drive-By Peace educational program aimed at city youth from diverse socioeconomic backgrounds.

Diana Grams, executive director of the Peace Museum, explains that through drawings, poetry, and essays on peace, children discover how to resolve conflicts peacefully. "Creativity," she says, "is the key source of power, for creativity delivers alternative solutions, and that is what conflict resolution and problem solving is all about."

To Grams, art is not passive. It is about action — heartfelt action. "During my education I was taught that the purpose of art is just for art's sake," she says. "I don't believe that. I think art should be part of the community, part of all our lives."

EDUCATORS CHANGE THEIR TUNE

The role of the arts in our schools has been hardest issue to address. When public schools face budget cuts, usually the first to go is the music program. Educators wouldn't dream of dropping math or science classes, yet recent studies indicate that music training can enhance spatial-temporal reasoning, the very type of intelligence required for high-level math and science. We're finally understanding the connection between the arts and the development of the human intellect, as well as the importance of educating the whole student. This groundbreaking research linking music to intellectual development was conducted at the University of California, Irvine, by neuroscientist Gordon Shaw and psychologist Frances Rauscher. One of their experiments involved college students who improved their scores on a spatial-temporal reasoning task after listening to a Mozart sonata. (Test scores showed no improvement when the same students listened to a relaxation tape or silence.)

These researchers then decided to determine if *studying* music, rather than just listening to it, can expand mental ability. In another experiment they offered private piano lessons, plus group singing sessions, to preschool children for a period of eight months. The researchers tested the children's spatial reasoning skills before, during, and after the musical instruction. They compared these test results with children who didn't receive music lessons but attended the same preschool programs. One control group was given computer lessons instead of music, and although the children were fascinated with the computers, in the end it was not technology but the sound of music — specifically performing music — that dramatically demonstrated an increase in spatial-temporal reasoning.

These experiments suggest, says Shaw, that if you start musical training at an early age, when a child's cortex is maturing and plastic, music can reinforce sophisticated cognitive reasoning abilities. The children who participated in their study didn't have any special talent in music, but as they learned how to play and sing, the lessons seemed to strengthen the links between brain neurons, developing cortical firing patterns responsible for higher brain functions.

Shaw feels the results of their experiments have enormous educational implications, but he also says they have only just begun to map the relationship between music and brain development. "We suspect there are a lot more benefits to music that we haven't been able to show yet," he says.

Jane Alexander, the former chairman of the NEA, also points out that children who attend art classes score up to fifty points higher than their peers on both the verbal and math sections of the SAT.

Along with the practical value of higher SAT scores, Alexander stresses an invaluable side effect of the arts. "When we neglect the life of the spirit, we tempt fate to give us spiritless children."

"I CAN'T SING," "I CAN'T DANCE," "I CAN'T — "

One reason why the arts aren't more integrated into our everyday lives is the distinction made between those who believe themselves artistic and those who don't. We're usually placed in one of these categories by other people — teachers, parents, friends, critics, or any opinionated adult who feels the "duty" to serve as arbiter of talent.

Admittedly there are degrees of talent, and not all of us can gain fame or recognition for our artistic attempts, but the ability to explore the terrain of art is open to all. There has been too much focus on the arts as a performance-oriented goal, and not as a vital extension of our personalities. When we shut out different forms of self-expression, we turn our back on a creative reservoir that can make all the difference to the quality of our lives.

Imagine a life without imagination. This is not a theoretical dilemma. Many children and adults become stuck in linear thinking, rarely taking the detours offered by the inward eye. Richard Lewis is the executive director of the Touchstone Center, a non-profit educational organization based in New York that conducts workshops to teach people why cultivating the imagination is needed to benefit all individuals.

"I think we have to redefine what we mean by imagination," says Lewis. "People define imagination as the fantasy part of themselves, or the part they make things up with. They don't think of it in terms of giving meaning to life, as something integral and central to who they are."

Any human without severe neurological problems can create an image, continues Lewis, and he encourages people to look outward and inward simultaneously to absorb this point: "The eye doesn't simply look out. It is attached to the deeper part of ourselves, and what we are feeling and seeing inwardly affects what we see outwardly. So in large part, the imagination has a great deal to do with the nature of perception — how we perceive anything in life."

One of Lewis's favorite words is insight. "It's the sight we have perceived from the inner part of ourselves," he says. "The power of the imagination allows the individual to ultimately make some sense of the world."

THE ARTS AS A SPIRITUAL PATHWAY

Making greater use of our imagination is only the beginning. How about playing an instrument? How about singing? David Darling, a cellist, composer, and international recording artist, delivers the same vehement message as Lewis: Creativity is a person's birthright. Darling founded Music for People, an educational foundation that turns playing music into "play" — enjoyable, accessible, a form of expression available to everyone, not just a chosen few.

His approach attempts to counteract the popular opinion that you can't play unless you've had lessons, or are working to be really accomplished. Our excessive concern about the right notes and wrong notes, believes Darling, has prevented too many of us from singing in public, from experimenting with an instrument, and from being spontaneous. "In the Western hemisphere," he says, "we've done a wonderful job of turning people off to music because we've made it such a narrow ball game to be successful in, but I believe we are all musical. It makes me mad when people say, 'I can't sing.' What do you mean you can't sing? You can walk, talk. Don't be a spectator. Sing your own song."

Darling's hope is that others can enjoy what he has gained from music. "All my life music has meant so much to me in a spiritual way," he says, "and I don't mean that in a corny way."

It may sound corny to say that a great symphony can stir the soul but the fact remains that it does. To Darling, music needn't attain the level of Beethoven or Brahms to affect us. The act of listening, playing, or participating in music at any level, he says, can elevate the human spirit. "I have always felt that if I can understand that, how come everybody doesn't?" Darling asks. "It takes no special talent. It just takes a certain environment where people are exposed in a benevolent way to music and to the energy involved."

In a similar vein, musician and dancer Gabrielle Roth exhorts, "Everybody — every BODY — needs to move." Through her workshops and tapes, Roth prods life into leaden bodies by first telling people that it is unnatural not to move. When she looks at the human being, she focuses on the "being," seeing all existence as a fluid state — as rhythm. "That's not esoteric," she reasons. "It's physics. If everything is in motion in the universe why make an exception of ourselves?"

Yet why dance? Why not just walk, run, exercise? Because when you dance, says Roth, you can actually move people with movement. Move them away from being inflexible, not just physically but also emotionally. She, too, speaks about the spiritual effect. When the dance becomes more than just fancy steps, explains Roth, when it becomes a passionate outlet for releasing tensions and feelings, it frees not only the body but the soul.

"With dance there is no separation," she says. "A painter has a brush and canvas, a writer has a piece of paper, and a musician has an instrument. A dancer is the instrument. There is no distance. Dance is the most personal of the art forms in that respect. And when the body, heart, and mind are unified through dance, then that is an expression of the soul."

TRANSFORMING LIVES

One of the most eloquent voices on how the arts touch the human spirit is Benjamin Zander, conductor of the Boston

Philharmonic Orchestra and Boston's Youth Philharmonic Orchestra. In recent years, Zander has found himself on the international lecture circuit, talking to leaders in many countries about the transformational power of music. The BBC produced a one hour documentary on Zander's work called *Living on One Buttock* — an odd title unless you have seen Zander move his body when he plays the piano or the cello, or watched him teach a student who is playing an instrument stiffly how to release inhibitions and emotions until her whole mind and body stretches and unites with the music.

"If you sit firmly on two buttocks," explains Zander, who displays a contagious enthusiasm for music, "the music tends to stay flat or rooted. When you play, you have to literally lift off — at least inside! When you do, so does the audience."

He tells the story of flying over England and looking down at the patchwork quilt of the English countryside, marked by fences around squares of green fields. He offers this analogy: "For the sheep in the field, the fence may be important, but the hawk can fly above it all. The artists are the hawks. We enable people to think beyond the fences in their lives. Our job is to lift people up and out of their normal ways of thinking, living, and being, and transport them."

However, he also emphasizes that music is a force bigger than any one musician: "I think the composers themselves, with few exceptions, would be the first to say that music is about something bigger than we are as individuals. Beethoven was certainly not saying, 'Listen to me. This is all about me.' He was saying this is about the brotherhood of man.

"There are performers," he continues, "who get stuck on themselves, and they put a barrier between themselves and the true beauty and impact of the music reaching the audience. So it's all about giving up oneself. It's a hard concept for musicians to understand. We often think it's about us, which is why we become anxious and nervous when we play."

Zander is a professor of music at the New England Conservatory, the artistic director of the New England Conservatory music program at Walnut Hill, and also a visiting professor at the Royal College of Music in London. He has taught master classes all over the world, and knows the importance of music in the educational system. "Music is one of the best ways of enabling people to get in touch with their emotions in a spiritually uplifting, nonverbal way," he says. "It brings into play feelings, relationships, and experiences not available under normal circumstances, through normal communication. The greater the music, the greater the power it has to transform lives. The schools are not taking advantage of this transformational power when they reduce arts in the classroom. Three thousand years ago Plato said that music was one of only three crucial elements in education. To take music away from young children is to take away part of their humanity."

Another well-known musician, Scott Singer, who has won three Emmy awards for his television scores, feels that young children, even before they enter school, should be taught to open up their senses. "The blockage of our senses is the first crime," asserts Singer. "You can't appreciate art unless you learn how to look, listen, smell. For example, teach a child to close their eyes and track with their ears a bird flying above, or listen to a bumblebee."

The vibrational level of music, he adds, is the spark that ignites the senses. "If you were watching a film and heard a tremendous explosion, you would absolutely *feel* that explosion. But if the audio was cut off, and you're simply seeing the explosion, you might feel detached."

The role of the musician, maintains Singer, is to expose the emotions until it's impossible for the listener to be detached. "If you're emotionally inclined like Beethoven," he says, "you have a lot of angst; you release the anger through music, until the music pours out with fury, pain, and intensity. Typically, that is the first movement. For example, in Beethoven's Pathetique Sonata in C minor, the first movement has these big, thick, minor chords. It's full of anger and passion, as he expresses his longing for the type of love he wants in his life. Then, after the first movement, he has a chance to heal — heal himself, as well as heal the listener. So the second movement is pure love. It is simple, flowing, and every note is designed to massage the soul — to caress you. This is what makes this kind of music last hundreds of years."

Today, Singer says, much of modern music is stuck in the first movement. "If you listen to rap music, you realize the rappers are angry with a society where the streets are crowded with drugs and violence. We all have to get to the second movement, because the tension is just building, building."

To Scott Singer, it's the musician who can move society into the second movement, where love and healing can flow naturally.

HEALING THROUGH THE ARTS

That the arts can help heal a society is an ethereal, hard-to-grasp concept. But the long-acknowledged potential of the arts to heal broken spirits is now extending into a potential to heal broken bodies. At the Harlem Hospital Trauma Center in New York, they regularly treat children who have been traumatized by serious accidents — falls, car accidents, gunshots. In the midst of this urban turmoil and human suffering is a remarkable oasis: an art studio that offers young children and adolescents the chance not just to paint but to reframe their lives.

Bill Richards, who heads the art studio, says that the art classes help traumatized kids — in-patients as well as community children — transfer their deepest emotions to canvas. The studio avoids formal instruction so that the kids have the freedom to experiment and find their own answers, without worrying about making mistakes. Richards is convinced that this freedom from judgment and the chance to express one's own individuality serve as a catalyst for self-healing. Several of the youngsters' paintings have been so impressive they have been exhibited professionally, but the purpose of the art goes beyond hanging on walls.

Richards remembers the day when Abraham Daniel arrived at the art studio. At age nine, Daniel had fallen three stories, following a dare by school friends to climb a scaffold. He severely injured his spine, and was comatose for over a month. The accident left him a quadriplegic, and his mother was told he would never walk again. When Daniel first arrived at the art studio, the young boy's muscles shook so fiercely he could hardly hold a paint brush.

"He had determination and a great need for self-expression," Richards recalls. "Painting became an immediate obsession, and by working with intense focus and concentration, he began to show improvement in his motor control."

Daniel tackled his paintings from a wheelchair, but one day Richards presented him with a canvas that was too large for him to complete from a sitting position. "I wondered what would happen if I put a seven-foot by five-foot canvas in front of this youngster," he says. "He was absolutely awed by the size and very anxious to work on it."

Daniel started by painting the bottom half of the canvas. He stretched his arms up as far as he could from his wheelchair and then stopped, but not for long. With all the energy he could muster, he pushed himself up from his chair and clung to the top edge of the canvas. "He held onto that edge and stood there shaking and painting," says Richards. "When he was finished he hobbled to the bathroom."

Since that day, Daniel no longer needs a wheelchair. In chapter 2, physicians discussed how our state of mind can alter the state of our body, but how can the act of painting a picture heal a person physically? Richards, who has witnessed other extraordinary instances of children being transformed physically and emotionally through art, offers this answer, "The act of creation is an incredible vehicle for the mind to inform the body of its completeness, of its wholeness. Essentially that is what art does. So in a sense, when somebody is disabled, perhaps it enhances that need for creating wholeness."

Through art, continues Richards, it is possible — on a conscious and subconscious level — to view life's various fragments, with all its contradictions, and somehow reconcile and unify these elements. "Abraham," he says, "is a classic example of a unified mind, body, and psyche identifying with the completeness of his painted images."

Neurologist Oliver Sacks, whose inspiring work with patients with severe brain disorders is documented in *Awakenings* and other bestselling books, has also observed the power of the arts. One of his patients was an elderly woman who couldn't speak but was suddenly able to sing when she heard music. When the music stopped, her voice stopped; only music could activate the speech center in her brain. But why this happens in these patients remains a mystery.

THE ARTS AS THERAPY

Today, the arts are also being used more and more as a therapeutic tool, delivering catharsis and illumination. Both art and music therapy are relatively new professions, but they are already having a profound impact in the world of healing.

A pioneer in the music therapy movement is Dr. Helen Bonny who founded the Institute for Consciousness and Music in the 1970s (now called The Bonny Foundation). She began this movement after conducting research at the Maryland Psychiatric Research Center exploring music's effect on the response to psychedelic drugs. These experiments revealed that when participants listened to music while in a drug-induced state, they felt a sense of safety, which then made it easier to explore altered states of consciousness.

This research convinced Bonny of music's therapeutic potential, but she also concluded that drugs weren't necessary to alter consciousness. Music by itself, she says, can naturally trigger memories and evoke deep feelings. Eventually she developed a form of therapy, called Guided Imagery and Music, which delves into the human psyche, using music, visualization, and relaxation techniques.

This form of therapy has now been adopted on a clinical level to assist clients with physical and emotional problems. In addition, it can help people who desire a dynamic medium for personal self-exploration, but there is also another effect. Bonny and other music therapists have noticed that as their clients travel with music into unexplored areas of the self, spiritual questions automatically surface. "The arts," believes Bonny, "are a natural conduit for shifting a person into a higher state of awareness about themselves and about the universe."

She once told the physicians of the American Holistic Medical Association, "As medicine moves toward holism, integrating mind, body, and spirit, it moves closer to music, which has always captured man's total beingness."

A worldwide organization called Music Therapists for Peace has also been established to show how music can bridge differences and affirm commonalities. Founded by Edith Hillman

Boxill in the United States, this organization has taken music therapy beyond the treatment room, introducing their methodology to educators, conflict resolution groups, and national and international peace organizations. Music therapists develop specific skills to reach people on a nonverbal level, using music from many different cultures. In any country, and any setting, they know how to bring people together through songs that have universal appeal, or by playing instruments that are indigenous to practically every country, such as drums.

Boxill explains one of their techniques: "We take people who see themselves as individuals, and we bring them together as a unified group by having them lock into the same pulse. We ask them to chant the same chant, or do a drumming circle for peace. In the beginning they move to their own rhythm but very quickly they pick up the same rhythm as their neighbor, louder and louder, until they are moving and responding to the same pulse, all in sympathetic vibration. It is like two violins vibrating in unity. Music therapy is an experiential medium. Once they have participated in this process, and made contact with each other, it can have a lasting effect. Music is the one natural medium that links us together."

Music Therapists for Peace also runs a project called Students Against Violence Everywhere through Music Therapy (SAVE), which is designed to reduce violence in the schools. Again, the concept is to release pent-up emotions by introducing *literally* harmonious ways of acting through music. Their goal is the same as the Drive-by Peace arts educational program mentioned earlier; they provide positive alternatives to destructive behavior.

DELIVERING THE BEST AND THE WORST

Today, whenever we hear about destructive behavior, blaming fingers point to the entertainment industry. Are children killing children because their emotions have been numbed by watching countless acts of violence on TV? Many feel that inane plots filled with gruesome violence are eroding minds and morality. The entertainment industry has reacted by arguing that in an uncensored society people must be free to produce what they wish and audiences should avoid material they might find offensive.

What Hollywood and the TV industry are wrestling with are the same questions regarding social responsibility faced by every corporation today. Unfortunately, explicit sex and violence sells. When the ratings go up for escapist drivel, profits do too.

"Our culture is controlled by numbers," decries Norman Lear, who believes our entire society has become hostage to numerical judgments, whether they are Neilson ratings, box office grosses, SAT scores, or political polls. In the '50s, Lear participated in the first live television broadcasts from coast to coast, made possible by transcontinental TV cables. Over the years, he has seen technology greatly improve, but he is dismayed at the small advances in programming. Television, he says, has not lived up to its full potential, and he places most of the blame on allowing quantity, not quality, to dictate what is produced.

"Fifteen years ago the *New York Times* wasn't printing the top twenty shows, or telling you which network was in the lead," he says. "People stand in line to go to the movies and talk about how much money pictures have made. We are addicted to numbers. It is kind of a numerical imagination, instead of a spiritual imagination."

When Lear received the Educational Foundation Award of the National Association of Television Program Executives, he delivered this challenge to his colleagues: "How do we begin to break down that wall that separates our higher personal ideals from the conduct of our professional and daily lives? And wouldn't it be extraordinary if we in television, with our enormous impact on the culture, could take the lead in that?"

He added, "I am convinced that the Great American Viewing

Audience will be far better served the day you decide to drop the numbers-driven mental maps that lay claim to you now — in favor of developing those programs that flow solely from your tastes and sensibilities, from your capacities for awe and wonder and mystery — and from your humanity and compassion — and from that voice within you that may be saying even now — 'this is right, this is right.'"

When it is right it doesn't happen by chance. Every artist will acknowledge, whether working in TV, the theater, a night club, or at a computer stringing words, that it takes years of dedication and practice to create worthy art.

World-renowned vibraphonist Bobby Hutcherson sums up his reaction to the artistic process this way: "I must prepare myself as much as possible for the music to come through me. I have to practice. I have to prepare mentally. I have to be an honest person. I get to unzip my body and explore my feelings, my emotions. If it goes the way it is supposed to, I will be just as amazed as the audience at what is happening. I give my music until it is just so overwhelming that it is a selfish thing to do — selfish for everyone. At that point it runs over. You can't destroy it. You can't do a thing about it, and neither can I."

The arts record and remind us of beauty, as well as evil; they help us see life with such clarity that we come away shocked, inspired, or both. The arts dig into the inner life, and their spiritual function is irreplaceable. They not only activate our senses, but let us live fully in this world by awakening — through the creative spirit — the human spirit.

Above all, art is a vehicle for transformation, the most potent medium on earth for transforming our souls. A reminder about how other cultures see the connections between the arts and other parts of their lives is summed up by arts therapist Phoebe Farris-Dufrene, who is part Powhatan American Indian. "Native Americans regard art as an element of life, not as a separate aesthetic ideal," she writes. "In Aboriginal societies, the arts are aspects of public life, which bring together dancing, poetry, the plastic and graphic arts into a single function: ritual as the all-embracing expression. Art is indispensable to ritual, and ritual is the native American concept of the whole life process. Native people see painting as indistinct from dancing, dancing as indistinct from worship, and worship as indistinct from living."

CHAPTER EIGHT

Toward a More Unified,
Compassionate Society

The best news about this book is what it doesn't include. There isn't space in this volume to profile all the groups who are working with selfless dedication to improve society. The tandem task of transforming ourselves and the world suffers neither from a shortage of ideas nor a shortage of individuals willing to donate time and energy. It is this massive effort that is the most encouraging sign of all.

People are banding together to improve the environment, our health system, and our educational system. Activists are calling our attention to those in desperate need: the elderly, the poor, our children. Groups are finding new approaches to racial issues and women's issues. Experts are teaching others how to resolve conflict, how to enhance relationships. Workshops and conferences devoted to personal and spiritual growth are appearing everywhere. The choices and opportunities for social change have never been so great.

So why do we seem stuck? Why is there still so much pessimism? Perhaps it is because the cloud that hangs over our civilization obscures the small successes; we are waiting for a bold breakthrough without realizing we already know what to do.

Our gloom has ample reason. Although we may blame the media for delivering so much bad news, our newspapers and newsmagazines are filled with very legitimate problems. Our wake-up call for change went off years ago, and has been getting louder and louder.

While we have all heard the alarm, many have turned it off and continue sleep-walking. We mustn't lose sight, however, of the many others who have responded to these crises with vigor. The gravity of the problems — environmental threats, economic insecurity, the escalation of violence — has forced millions to reevaluate how they are running their lives and how their leaders are running their countries.

We have experienced impressive leaps forward. The movement for ecological sustainability has motivated many corporations to become more socially responsible, and compelled many to reject the materialistic lifestyle. Whole-person medicine has helped other disciplines accept a whole-systems approach. And the technology of the internet has closed the space between cultures and countries at a time when scientists are confirming that all life is interdependent and interrelated. Above all, people are earnestly searching for meaning and purpose — anything to make sense of it all.

Unfortunately, we tend to ridicule or trivialize seekers looking for inner peace, or those trying to apply the power of love to solve societal problems. We've become so accustomed to hard news, we make light of anything soft.

Yet what could be more important than discovering we're more empathetic or altruistic than we thought, or that the human heart really does dictate messages to the brain? What could be more exciting than the world's religions overcoming differences in faith to work together for the benefit of humankind? What is more hopeful than the Natural Step concept, where people are also working together to build a consensual framework for sustainability? What is more necessary than flexible work schedules and shorter hours so we can lead a balanced, fulfilling life?

The most conspicuous absence in these chapters is the role politics plays in this new vision of the world. Currently the majority of politicians are part of the problem, not part of the solution, mainly because they remain trapped in the ruthless mentality of campaigning. Political actions still fall prey to the interests of greed and power and fail in sharing resources and developing policies for the greater good.

While researching this book, I hoped to prove that all the positive signs would add up to the inevitable transformation of society. My optimism was soon dampened by realism. Western society has made many commendable moves in the right direction, but remains on the verge of a drastic wrong turn. Sociologist Paul Ray has reached the same conclusion. Even though his research identified a population of 44 million idealistic individuals who strongly support ecological sustainability and other social concerns, he says, "In the next two decades our world will either be dramatically better or dramatically worse. The one thing that cannot happen is just 'more of the same.' Most trends of the past are simply not sustainable. The era of obvious steps to progress is gone, and we face the Great Divide. It really could go either way: Our future is not foreordained. We are at a tipping point in civilization."

Nevertheless, as this book illustrates, throughout society we are beginning to develop practical and effective ways to promote the best in human nature. Admittedly, many pieces in this jigsaw puzzle of societal transformation are still missing, but even with just the pieces already in place we can start to see a brighter future.

Which leads to a final story. Each year an international panel of environmental experts selects a handful of ecological crusaders from around the world to receive the prestigious Goldman Environmental Prize. One year, Wangari Muta Maathai, a professor in Kenya, was a winner. She had initiated a tree planting project in East Africa to curtail deforestation and desertification. Her grassroots group, comprised mainly of women, became renowned as the Green Belt Movement. Maathai also managed to stop the construction of a sixty-story skyscraper in the middle of Nairobi's largest public open space. The Kenyan government at the time labeled her "subversive," and she was arrested and detained.

I talked to Maathai when she came to the United States to receive her prize. "I don't have any special talent," she said modestly. "I just felt the urge to do something, and I always tell people you must pursue that urge."

She paused, making this final statement, followed by joyous laughter: "When we say that an individual can make a difference, the truth of the matter is that everyone is making a difference. In the final analysis all of us are doing something or not doing something. It all depends which side we are on."

NOTES

Information in the text is based on personal interviews with the author, as well as the following sources, referenced by page number and key phrases.

INTRODUCTION
Toward Wholeness: Connecting the Heart, Conscience, and Spirit

xvii   **Whole-system view of things.** Duane Elgin, "Global Paradigm Change: Is a Shift Underway?" (an overview report to the State of the World Forum, San Francisco, California, 1996).

xvii   **Despite the economic problems.** Ibid., p. 5.

xvii   **Compared to the rest of society.** Paul H. Ray, "The Rise of Integral Culture" (a survey cosponsored by the Fetzer Institute and the Institute of Noetic Sciences, printed in *Noetic Sciences Review*, Spring 1996, No. 37).

xviii **Bigger than any comparable group**. Ibid.

xix **I consider it to be the major failure of my public life.** Elizabeth Shogren, "Clinton Lauds Courage of Fight Against Apartheid," *Los Angeles Times*, March 29, 1998.

xix **Spiritual dimension that connects all cultures.** Address of the president of the Czech Republic, Vaclav Havel, on the occasion of Jackson H. Ralston Prize Ceremony, Stanford University, September 29, 1994.

xix **If democracy is to spread successfully throughout the world.** Ibid.

CHAPTER ONE
Building a Connection between Spirituality and Science

6 **A careful observer of the world's religions today**. Diana Eck, speech at an Interfaith Conference, Rediscovering Justice, University of San Francisco, California, June 22, 1995.

6 **London is now part of the Muslim world.** Ibid.

6 **If I tolerate you.** Ibid.

10 **Ending hunger is more than digging wells.** Joan Holmes, speech at Windstar's 1987 Choices for the Future Symposium, Snowmass, Colorado.

12 **Our definitions of progress.** Gerald O. Barney, with Jane Blewett and Kristen R. Barney, *Global 2000 Revisited: What Shall We Do?* Millennium Institute, 1993.

12 **Some of my colleagues.** Acceptance speech of Professor Paul Davies, upon receiving the Templeton Prize for Progress in Religion, at Westminster Abbey, London, May 3, 1995.

12 **Whatever the universe as a whole may be about.** Ibid.

12 **We still haven't a clue.** Ibid.

15 **May provide the foundation.** Henry P. Stapp, "Values and the Quantum Conception of Man" (paper presented at UNESCO sponsored symposium "Science and Culture: A Common Path for the Future," Tokyo, September 1995).

17   **The world has suffered.** Brian D. Josephson and Beverly A. Rubik, "The Challenge of Consciousness Research," *Frontier Perspectives*, Vol. 3, No. 1, Fall 1992, p. 18. (See article on http://www.tcm.phy.cam.ac.uk/~bdj10/mm/articles/athens.html.)

17   **The new science.** Ibid., p. 19.

18   **We must not allow this territory.** Norman Lear, speech to the National Press Club, Washington, D.C., December 9, 1993.

18   **It is a buzzing, disconnected eruption.** Ibid.

CHAPTER TWO
The Caring Connection

23   **The question of whether we care for others.** C. Daniel Batson, "How Social an Animal? The Human Capacity for Caring," *American Psychologist*, The American Psychological Association, Inc., March 1990, p. 336.

24   **Lest we feel too much.** Ibid., p. 344.

24   **Could this apparent necessity to defend ourselves.** Ibid.

24   **Fragile flower of altruistic caring.** Ibid., p. 345.

24   **Before we can do this.** Ibid.

25   **The prefrontal cortex is the only neocortex.** Paul D. MacLean, M.D., "A Mind of Three Minds: Educating the Triune Brain," in J.S. Chall and A.F. Mirsky, eds. *The Seventy-Seventh Yearbook of the National Society for the Study of Education* (Chicago: University of Chicago Press, 1978), p. 340.

25   **Why, slowly but progressively.** Ibid.

26   **Trusting hearts last longer.** Redford Williams, *The Trusting Heart* (New York: Times Books, 1989).

29   **We must consider the possibility.** Paul D. MacLean, M.D., "The Brain in Relation to Empathy and Medical Education," *The Journal of Nervous and Mental Disease*, Vol. 144, 1967, p. 374.

31   **I am suggesting.** Ervin Staub, "The Evolution of Caring and Nonaggressive Persons and Societies," *Journal of Social Issues*, Vol. 44, No. 2, 1988, p. 88.

31   **Suppose one is deciding.** Martin L. Hoffman, "Empathic Emotions and Justice in Society," a paper, p. 25.

33   **The answer must include a motive.** Ibid.., 34.

37   **A recent study by the Department of Justice.** BJS statistician Caroline Wolf Harlow, "Profile of Jail Inmates 1996," a survey by the Bureau of Justice Statistics. For copies contact (301) 519-5550, document 111; website http://www.ojp.usdoj.gov/bjs/.

42   **Helping other people.** Dalai Lama, speech at the Commonwealth Club of California, October 10, 1989.

CHAPTER THREE
Healing Ourselves to Heal Society

46   **In the beginning of my work.** Candace Pert, "Neuropeptides: The Emotions and Bodymind," *Noetic Sciences Review*, Spring 1987, p.16. Article adapted by Harris Dienstfrey from a talk by Pert at the Symposium on Consciousness and Survival, sponsored by the Institute of Noetic Sciences, October 25–26, 1985; reprinted with permission from *Advances*, Vol. 3, No. 3, Summer 1986, Institute for the Advancement of Health.

47   **I think it is possible.** Ibid., p. 18.

50   **Love and intimacy are at a root of what makes us sick.** Dean Ornish, *Love and Survival: The Scientific Basis for the Healing Power of Intimacy* (New York: HarperCollins, 1998), p. 3.

54   **No informed person at this point.** Gail Bernice Holland, "A Conversation with Russell Targ and Jane Kantra," *Connections Magazine*, February 1998.

54   **The most profound implications.** Marilyn J. Schlitz, "Intentionality: An Argument for Transpersonal Consciousness," *World Futures* 1997, Vol. 48, pp. 115-126; Overseas Publishers Association, Amsterdam, B.V. Published in the Netherlands under license by Gordon and Breach Science Publishers.

63   **Same procedure, different intent.** Janet Quinn, "Therapeutic Touch: The Empowerment of Love," *New Realities*, May/June 1987, p. 26.

63   **Extend beyond the care-giving context.** Ibid.., p. 25.
63   **Thus, the old adage.** Ibid.., p. 26.
64   **What would the effect be.** Ibid.
65   **It's about uncovering.** Rachel Naomi Remen, M.D., "The Recovery of the Sacred, Part 1," *Unity Magazine*, October 1995, p. 9.

CHAPTER FOUR
Working to Benefit Society

68   **More than 43 million jobs have been lost.** "The Downsizing of America," *The New York Times*, March 3, 1996, p. 15.
68   **Whether the new technologies free us.** Jeremy Rifkin, *The End of Work: The Decline of the Global Labor Force and the Dawn of the Post-Market Era* (New York, A Jeremy P. Tarcher/Putnam Book, 1995), p. xvii.
69   **Ecosystem of society.** Harris Sussman, "Employment in the Next Millennium," paper, October 1990, p. 2.
69   **What's so difficult about work-family issues.** Harris Sussman, "Are We Talking Revolution?" *Across the Board*, July/August 1990, p. 25.
73   **The devastating effects that overwork is having.** Barbara Brandt, "Less Time for Our Jobs, More Time for Ourselves," paper, July 1991, p. 32.
73   **The results of this study.** "Report of the Advisory Group on Working Time and the Distribution of Work," Canadian Human Resources and Development, December 1994. For copies call (819) 997-2617.
74   **In practical terms this implies reduced working hours.** Report of the Advisory Group on Working Time and the Distribution of Work, December 1994, production coordinated by the Bureau of Labour Information and Communications (Programs) of Human Resources Development, Canada, p. 52.
76   **The GNP counts air pollution.** Robert F. Kennedy, "Recapturing America's Moral Vision," speech, March 18, 1968.

76   **A parent raising a child is engaged.** Ted Halstead and Clifford Cobb, "The Genuine Progress Indicator," Summary of Data and Methodology, September 1994.

78   **Eighty-two percent of those surveyed.** "Yearning for Balance: Views of Americans on Consumption, Materialism, and the Environment," July 1995. Prepared for the Merck Family Fund by The Harwood Group, p. 5.

88   **How do you ennoble the spirit.** Anita Roddick, *Body and Soul: Profits with Principles* (New York: Crown Publishers, 1991), p. 22.

CHAPTER FIVE
Whole Ways to Learn

93   **With basic research as a powerful ally.** Linda Campbell, "Whole Person Education," *In Context*, No. 18, Winter 1988.

100   **Moral mutants.** "Ethical Values, Attitudes, and Behaviors in American Schools," executive summary of survey by the Joseph and Edna Josephson Institute.

104   **One of the highest forms of mental ability.** Arthur Costa, *Developing Minds* (Alexandria, Virginia: Association for Supervision and Curriculum Development, 1985), p. 31.

CHAPTER SIX
The Environmental Connection

113   **No ecology — no economy.** Paul Downton, speech at 1990 First International Ecological City Conference, Berkeley, California, organized by Urban Ecology.

114   **It is crucial to recognize.** Fritjof Capra, "We Need a New Vision," *Utne Reader*, September/October 1990, p. 45.

114   **In fact, the more we study the situation.** Ibid., p. 45.

115   **We know what we have to do.** Lester R. Brown, *State of the World, 1993: A Worldwatch Institute Report on Progress Toward a Sustainable Society* (New York: W.W. Norton & Company, 1993), p. 21.

116 **The deepest difference between optimists.** Donella Meadows, Dennis L. Meadows, and Jørgen Randers, *Beyond the Limits: Confronting Global Collapse, Envisioning a Sustainable Future.* (White River Junction, VT: Chelsea Green, 1992), p. 233.

117 **The sustainability revolution will have to be.** Ibid.

118 **What can a new biology contribute.** Brian Goodwin, Jane Clark, and Alizon Yiangou, "The Generative Order of Life," *Beshara Magazine*, United Kingdom, Issue 12, Autumn/Winter 1990; reprinted *Noetic Sciences Review*, Spring/Summer 1991.

125 **Isolated organisms back together.** Robert Augros and George Stanciu, "The New Biology," *Noetic Sciences Review*, Winter 1989, p. 4.

CHAPTER SEVEN
Living as a Work of Art

132 **The role of the arts in all communities.** Michael Greene, "The Role of the Arts in Twenty-First Century Habitats," a speech at the Habitat II Conference, Istanbul, Turkey, June 3, 1996.

133 **These results put to rest.** Louis Harris, "Americans and the Arts VII — A Nationwide Survey on the Attitudes of the American People Toward the Arts," prepared for the American Council for the Arts, the National Assembly of Local Arts Agencies, June 1996.

133 **We have always heard.** Robert Commanday, "The Precious U.S. — Soviet Cultural Link," *San Francisco Chronicle*, February 12, 1989, p. 14.

133 **Music and dance were the principal communication.** Ibid.

135 **Under such difficult circumstances.** Martha Henderson, "Humanitas Special Report: Yugoslavia, Hungary, Poland, Czechoslovakia," *Humanitas International Newsletter*, 1989, No. 3, p. 4.

135 **Our revolution had a number of steps.** Vit Horejs and Bonnie Stein, "The New King of Absurdistan," *Village Voice*, Jan. 16, 1990, Vol. 35, No. 3, pp. 31–35.

135   **Sarajevo Philharmonic Orchestra.** Philip Smucker, "Music under fire in Sarajevo," *San Francisco Examiner,* January 21, 1996, p. A10.

138   **When we neglect the life of the spirit.** Jane Alexander, chairman of the National Endowment for the Arts, in a speech to the American Society of Newspaper Editors annual convention, Dallas, Texas, April 7, 1995.

146   **A classic example of a unified mind.** Bill Richards, "Art of Necessity," a Guide for Developing a Children's Art Program in Hospitals, Harlem Horizon Art Studio, 1991, p. 10.

147   **As medicine moves toward holism.** Milton Friedman, "Musically Induced Imagery," *New Realities,* January/February 1990, p. 17.

149   **How do we begin to break down that wall.** Norman Lear, "New Mental Maps for the Millennium," speech upon receiving the Educational Foundation Award of the National Association of Television Program Executives, January 26, 1955.

149   **I am convinced that the Great American Viewing Audience.** Ibid.

150   **Native Americans regard art.** Phoebe Farris-Dufrene, "Utilizing the Arts for Healing from a Native American Perspective: Implications for Creative Arts Therapies," *The Canadian Journal of Native Studies,* Vol. X, No. 1, 1990, pp. 122–123.

CHAPTER EIGHT
Toward a More Unified, Compassionate Society

155   **In the next two decades.** Paul H. Ray, "The Rise of Integral Culture," a survey cosponsored by the Fetzer Institute and the Institute of Noetic Sciences, *Noetic Sciences Review,* Spring 1996.

SELECTED BIBLIOGRAPHY

RECOMMENDED HOLISTIC BOOKS

Arrien, Angeles. *The Four-Fold Way: Walking the Paths of the Warrior, Teacher, Healer and Visionary.* New York: HarperCollins, 1993.

Baldwin, Christina. *Calling the Circle: The First and Future Culture.* New York: Bantam, 1998.

Capra, Fritjof. *The Turning Point: Science, Society, and the Rising Culture.* New York: Simon & Schuster, 1982.

Eisler, Riane. *The Chalice and the Blade: Our History, Our Future.* San Francisco: HarperCollins, 1987.

Eisler, Riane, and David Loye. *The Partnership Way: New Tools for Living and Learning.* San Francisco: HarperCollins, 1990.

Elgin, Duane. *Awakening Earth: Exploring the Evolution of Human Culture and Consciousness.* New York: Morrow, 1993.

Elgin, Duane. *Voluntary Simplicity.* New York: Morrow, 1993.

Ehrlich, Paul R., Anne H. Ehrlich, and Gretchen D. Daily. *The Stork and the Plow: The Equity Answer to the Human Dilemma.* New York: Putnam, 1995.

Ferguson, Marilyn. *The Aquarian Conspiracy: Personal and Social Transformation in the 1980s.* Los Angeles: Tarcher, 1987.

Harding, Vincent. *Hope and History: Why We Must Share the Story of the Movement.* New York: Orbis Books, 1991.

Harman, Willis. *Global Mind Change.* San Francisco: Institute of Noetic Sciences and Berrett-Koehler, 1998.

Heckler, Richard. *Crossings: Everyday People, Extraordinary Events, & Life-Affirming Change.* New York: Harcourt Brace, 1998.

Hubbard, Barbara Marx. *Conscious Evolution: Awakening Our Social Potential.* Novato, Calif.: New World Library, 1998.

Lappé, Frances Moore, and Paul Martin DuBois. *The Quickening of America: Rebuilding Our Nation, Remaking Our Lives.* San Francisco: Jossey-Bass, 1994.

Lemkow, Anna F. *The Wholeness Principle: Dynamics of Unity Within Science, Religion & Society.* Wheaton, Ill.: Quest Books, 1990.

Leonard, George, and Michael Murphy. *The Life We Are Given: A Long-Term Program for Realizing the Potential of Body, Mind, Heart, and Soul.* New York: Tarcher/Putnam, 1995.

Leonard, George. *The Transformation: A Guide to the Inevitable Changes in Humankind.* New York: Delta, 1973.

Lerner, Michael. *The Politics of Meaning: Restoring Hope and Possibility in an Age of Cynicism.* Reading, Mass.: Addison-Wesley, 1996.

Levey, Joel and Michelle Levey. *Living in Balance: A Dynamic Approach for Creating Harmony & Wholeness in a Chaotic World.* Berkeley, Calif.: Conari, 1998.

Marshall, Joseph Jr. *Street Soldier.* New York: Delacorte Press, 1996.

McLaughlin, Corrine, and Gordon Davidson. *Spiritual Politics: Changing the World from the Inside Out.* New York: Ballantine, 1994.

Mische, Gerald, and Patricia Mische. *Toward a Human World Order: Beyond the National Security Straitjacket.* New York: Paulist Press, 1977.

Mishlove, Jeffrey. *Thinking Allowed: Conversations On the Leading Edge of Knowledge.* Tulsa, Okla.: Council Oak Books, 1992.

Ornstein, Robert, and Richard Thompson. *New World, New Mind.* New York: Simon & Schuster, 1990.

Prothrow-Stith, Deborah, with Michael Weissman: *Deadly Consequences: How Violence Is Destroying Our Teenage Population and a Plan to Begin Solving the Problem.* New York: HarperCollins, 1991.

Russell, Peter. *The Global Brain Awakens: Our Next Evolutionary Leap.* Palo Alto, Calif.: Global Brain, 1995.

Schumacher, E.F. *Small Is Beautiful: Economics as if People Mattered.* New York: Harper & Row, 1973.

Smith, Hedrick, *Rethinking America.* New York: Random House, 1995.

Spretnak, Charlene. *The Resurgence of the Real: Body, Nature and Place in a Hypermodern World.* Reading, Mass.: Addison-Wesley, 1997

West, Cornel. *Race Matters.* New York: Vintage Books, 1994.

Wallis, Jim. *The Soul of Politics: Beyond "Religious Right" and "Secular Left."* New York: The New Press, 1994.

Wilber, Ken. *A Brief History of Everything.* Boston: Shambhala, 1996.

Wilber, Ken. *Sex, Ecology, Spirituality: The Spirit of Evolution.* Boston: Shambhala, 1995.

Williamson, Marianne. *The Healing of America.* New York: Simon & Schuster, 1997.

BUILDING A CONNECTION BETWEEN SPIRITUALITY AND SCIENCE

Becker, Robert, and Gary Selden. *The Body Electric: Electromagnetism and the Foundation of Life.* New York: Morrow, 1987.

Bohm, David. *Wholeness and the Implicate Order.* Boston: Routledge, 1980.

Bohm, David, and F. David Peat. *Science, Order and Creativity.* New York: Bantam, 1987.

Capra, Fritjof. *The Tao of Physics: An Exploration of the Parallels Between Modern Physics and Eastern Mysticism.* Boston: Shambhala, 1991.

Capra, Fritjof. *The Web of Life: A New Scientific Understanding of Living Systems*. New York: Anchor, 1996.

Davies, Paul. *God and the New Physics*. New York: Simon & Schuster, 1983.

Friedman, Norman. *Bridging Science and Spirit*. St. Louis, Mo.: Living Lake Books, 1994.

Goodwin, Brian. *How the Leopard Changed Its Spots: The Evolution of Complexity*. New York: Scribner's, 1994.

Goswami, Amit, with Maggi Goswami, and Richard E. Reed. *The Self-Aware Universe: How Consciousness Creates the Material World*. New York: Putnam, 1993.

Herbert, Nick. *Elemental Mind: Human Consciousness and the New Physics*. New York: Dutton, 1993.

Herbert, Nick. *Quantum Reality: Beyond the New Physics*. New York: Anchor/Doubleday, 1985.

Horgan, John. *The End of Science: Facing the Limits of Knowledge in the Twilight of the Scientific Age*. Reading, Mass.: Addison-Wesley, 1996.

Jahn, Robert G., and Brenda J. Dunne. *Margins of Reality: The Role of Consciousness in the Physical World*. New York: Harcourt Brace Jovanovich, 1987.

Larson, David B., and Susan S. Larson. *The Forgotten Factor in Physical and Mental Health: What Does the Research Show?* An Independent Study Seminar. National Institute for Healthcare Research, 6110 Executive Blvd., Suite 680, Rockville, MD 20952, 1995.

Pearce, Joseph Chilton. *Evolution's End: Claiming the Potential of Our Intelligence*. San Francisco: HarperSanFrancisco, 1992.

Radin, Dean. *The Conscious Universe: The Scientific Truth of Psychic Phenomena*. San Francisco: HarperSanFrancisco, 1997.

Sheldrake, Rupert. *Seven Experiments That Could Change the World: A Do-It-Yourself Guide to Revolutionary Science*. New York: Riverhead, 1995.

Sheldrake, Rupert. *The Presence of the Past: Morphic Resonance and the Habits of Nature*. New York: Times Books, 1988.

Sheldrake, Rupert, and Matthew Fox. *Natural Grace: Dialogues on Creation, Darkness, and the Soul in Spirituality and Science*. New York: Doubleday, 1996.

Sheldrake, Rupert, and Matthew Fox. *The Physics of Angels: Exploring the Realm Where Science and Spirit Meet.* San Francisco: HarperSanFrancisco, 1996.

Stevenson, Ian. *Where Reincarnation and Biology Intersect.* Westport, Conn.: Praeger, 1997.

Swimme, Brian. *The Hidden Heart of the Cosmos: Humanity and the New Story.* New York: Orbis, 1997.

Swimme, Brian, and Thomas Berry. *The Universe Story: From the Primordial Flaring Forth to the Ecozoic Era — A Celebration of the Unfolding of the Cosmos.* San Francisco: HarperSanFrancisco, 1992.

Targ, Russell and Jane Katra. *Miracles of Mind: Exploring Nonlocal Consciousness and Spiritual Healing.* Novato, Calif.: New World Library, 1998.

Templeton, John. *The Humble Approach: Scientists Discover God.* New York: Seabury Press, 1981.

Wilber, Ken. *The Marriage of Sense and Soul: Integrating Science and Religion.* New York: Random House, 1998.

Wolf, Fred Alan. *The Spiritual Universe: How Quantum Physics Proves the Existence of the Soul.* New York: Simon & Schuster, 1996.

Young, Arthur. *The Reflexive Universe: Evolution of Consciousness.* New York: Robert Briggs Associates, 1976.

Spiritual Books

Anderson, Sherry Ruth, and Patricia Hopkins. *The Feminine Face of God: The Unfolding of the Sacred in Women.* New York: Bantam, 1991.

Berman, Philip L. *The Journey Home: What Near-Death Experiences and Mysticism Teach Us About the Gift of Life.* New York: Pocket Books, 1996.

Beversluis, Joel, Editor. *A SourceBook for Earth's Community Religions.* Grand Rapids, Mich.: CoNexus Press; New York: Global Education Associates, 1995.

Boorstein, Sylvia. *It's Easier Than You Think: The Buddhist Way to Happiness.* San Francisco: HarperSanFrancisco, 1995.

Brussat, Frederic, and Mary Ann Brussat. *Spiritual Literacy: Reading the Sacred in Everyday Life.* New York: Scribner, 1996.

Carter, Jimmy. *Living Faith.* New York: Times Books, 1996.

Castelii, Jim, ed. *How I Pray: People of Different Religions Share with Us That Most Sacred and Intimate Act of Faith.* New York: Ballantine, 1994.

Catalfo, Phil. *Raising Spiritual Children in a Material World: Introducing Spirituality into Family Life.* New York: Berkley Books, 1997.

Chittister, Joan D. *A Passion for Life: Fragments of the Face of God.* New York: Orbis Books, 1996.

Chopra, Deepak. *The Path to Love: Renewing the Power of Spirit in Your Life.* New York: Harmony, 1997.

Das, Lama Surya. *Awakening the Buddha Within: Tibetan Wisdom for the Western World.* New York: Broadway Books, 1997.

Eck, Diana L. *Encountering God: A Spiritual Journey from Bozeman to Banaras.* Boston: Beacon Press, 1993.

Forward, Martin, ed. *Ultimate Visions: Reflections on the Religions We Choose.* New York: Oneworld Publications, 1995.

Grof, Christina. *The Stormy Search for the Self: A Guide to Personal Growth through Transformational Crises.* Los Angeles: Tarcher, 1990.

Grof, Christina, and Stanislav Grof. *Spiritual Emergency: When Personal Transformation Becomes a Crisis.* Los Angeles, New York: Tarcher, 1989.

Halifax, Joan. *The Fruitful Darkness: Reconnecting with the Body of the Earth.* San Francisco: HarperSanFrancisco, 1993.

Hanh, Thich Nhat. *Cultivating the Mind of Love: The Practice of Looking Deeply into Mahayana Buddhist Tradition.* Berkeley, Calif.: Parallax Press, 1996.

Hanh, Thich Nhat. *The Heart of the Buddha's Teaching: An Introduction to Buddhism.* Berkeley, Calif.: Parallax Press, 1996.

Hanh, Thich Nhat. *Living Buddha, Living Christ.* New York: Riverhead, 1995.

Hayden, Tom. *The Lost Gospel of the Earth: A Call for Renewing Nature, Spirit, and Politics.* San Francisco: Sierra Club Books, 1996.

Hillman, James. *The Soul's Code: In Search of Character and Calling.* New York: Random House, 1996.

His Holiness, the Dalai Lama. *Healing Anger: The Power of Patience from a Buddhist Perspective.* Ithaca, N.Y.: Snow Lion Publications, 1997.

Kabat-Zinn, Jon. *Wherever You Go, There You Are: Mindfulness Meditation in Everyday Life.* New York: Hyperion, 1994.

Kornfield, Jack. *A Path with Heart: A Guide through the Perils and Promises of Spiritual Life.* New York: Bantam, 1993.

Kornfield, Jack. *Living Dharma: Teachings of Twelve Buddhist Masters.* Boston: Shambhala Publications, 1996.

Lerner, Michael. *Jewish Renewal: A Path to Healing and Transformation.* New York: G.P. Putnam's Sons, 1994.

Lerner, Michael and Cornel West. *Jews and Blacks: Let the Healing Begin.* New York: Putnam, 1995.

Macy, Joanna. *World as Lover, World as Self.* Berkeley, Calif.: Parallax Press, 1991.

Mitchell, Stephen. *Genesis: A New Translation of the Classic Biblical Stories.* New York: HarperCollins, 1996.

Moore, Thomas. *Care of the Soul: A Guide for Cultivating Depth and Sacredness in Everyday Life.* New York: HarperCollins, 1992.

Moore, Thomas. *The Re-Enchantment of Everyday Life.* New York: HarperCollins, 1996.

Muller, Wayne. *How, Then, Shall We Live? Four Simple Questions that Reveal the Beauty and Meaning of Our Lives.* New York: Bantam, 1996.

Pearce, Joseph Chilton. *Evolution's End: Claiming the Potential of Our Intelligence.* San Francisco: HarperSanFrancisco, 1992.

Peck, Scott M. *The Road Less Traveled and Beyond: Spiritual Growth in an Age of Anxiety.* New York: Simon & Schuster, 1998.

Shield, Benjamin and Richard Carlson, eds. *For the Love of God: Handbook for the Spirit.* Novato, Calif.: New World Library, 1997.

Rinpoche, Sogyal. *The Tibetan Book of Living and Dying.* San Francisco: HarperSanFrancisco, 1992.

Thurman, Robert A. F. *Inner Revolution: Life, Liberty, and the Pursuit of Real Happiness.* New York: Riverhead/Putnam, 1998.

Trungpa, Chögyam. *Cutting Through Spiritual Materialism.* Boston: Shambhala, 1973.

Vardey, Lucinda, ed. *God in All Worlds: An Anthology of Contemporary Spiritual Writing.* New York: Pantheon, 1995.

Zaleski, Philip, and Paul Kaufman. *Gifts of the Spirit: Living the Wisdom of the Great Religious Traditions.* San Francisco: HarperSanFrancisco, 1997.

Zukav, Gary. *Seat of the Soul.* New York: Simon & Schuster, 1989.

THE CARING CONNECTION

Bennett. William J. *The Book of Virtues: A Treasury of Great Moral Stories.* New York: Simon & Schuster, 1993.

Borysenko, Joan. *Guilt Is the Teacher, Love Is the Lesson.* New York: Warner, 1990.

Canada, Geoffrey. *Fist Stick Knife Gun: A Personal History of Violence in America.* Boston: Beacon, 1995.

Carlson, Richard, and Benjamin Shield, eds. *Handbook for the Heart: Original Writings on Love.* New York: Little, Brown, 1996.

Cahill, Sedonia, Charles Garfield, and Cindy Spring. *Wisdom Circles: A Guide to Self-Discovery and Building Community in Small Groups.* New York: Hyperion, 1998.

Childre, Doc Lew. *Freeze-Frame: Fast Action Stress Relief.* Boulder Creek, Calif.: Planetary Publications, 1994.

Chopra, Deepak. *The Seven Spiritual Laws for Parents: Guiding Your Child to Success and Fulfillment.* New York: Harmony, 1997.

Counts, Alex. *Give Us Credit: How Muhammad Yunus's Micro-Lending Revolution Is Empowering Women from Bangladesh to Chicago.* New York: Times Books, 1996.

Csikszentmihalyi, Mihaly. *The Evolving Self.* New York: HarperCollins, 1993.

Damon, William. *Greater Expectations: Overcoming the Culture of Indulgence in Our Homes and Schools.* New York: Free Press, 1995.

Edelman, Marian Wright. *Guide My Feet: Prayers and Meditations on Loving and Working for Children.* Boston: Beacon Press, 1995.

Edelman, Marian Wright. *The Measure of Our Success: A Letter to My Children and Yours.* New York: Beacon Press, 1994.

Ellsworth, Robert, and Janet Ellsworth. *How Shall We Love?* New York: Putnam, 1996.

Etzioni, Amitai. *The Spirit of Community: The Reinvention of American Society.* New York: Simon & Schuster, 1994.

Goldhart, Stephen, and David Wallin. *Mapping the Terrain of the Heart: The Six Capacities That Guide the Journey of Love.* Reading, Mass.: Addison-Wesley, 1995.

Hillman, James. *The Soul's Code: In Search of Character and Calling.* New York: Random House, 1996.

Kabat-Zinn, Myla, and Jon Kabat-Zinn. *Everyday Blessings: The Inner Work of Mindful Parenting.* New York: Hyperion, 1997.

Keeney, Bradford. *Everyday Soul: Awakening the Spirit in Everyday Life.* New York: Riverhead, 1996.

Kohn, Alfie. *The Brighter Side of Human Nature: Altruism and Empathy in Everyday Life.* New York: Basic Books, 1990.

Kohn, Alfie. *Punished by Rewards: The Trouble with Gold Stars, Incentive Plans, A's, Praise and other Bribes.* New York: Houghton Mifflin, 1993.

Kornfield, Jack. *A Path with Heart: A Guide Through the Perils and Promises of Spiritual Life.* New York: Bantam, 1993.

Kornfield, Jack. *Soul Food: Stories to Nourish the Spirit and the Heart.* San Francisco: HarperSanFrancisco, 1996.

Kozol, Jonathan. *Amazing Grace: The Lives of Children and the Conscience of a Nation.* New York: Crown, 1995.

Levine, Stephen, and Ondrea Levine. *Embracing the Beloved: Relationship as a Path of Awakening.* New York: Doubleday, 1995.

Moore, Thomas. *The Education of the Heart.* New York: HarperCollins, 1996.

Needleman, Jacob. *Time and the Soul.* New York: Doubleday, 1998.

Shore, Bill. *Revolution of the Heart: A New Strategy for Creating Wealth and Meaningful Change.* New York: Riverhead Books, 1995.

Staub, Ervin. *The Roots of Evil: The Origins of Genocide and Other Group Violence.* New York: Cambridge University Press, 1989.

Welwood, John. *Love and Awakening: Discovering the Sacred Path of Intimate Relationship.* New York: HarperCollins, 1996.

Williams, Redford. *The Trusting Heart: Great News About Type A Behavior.* New York: Times Books, 1989.

Williams, Redford, and Virginia Williams. *Anger Kills: Seventeen Strategies for Controlling the Hostility That Can Harm Your Health.* New York: Times Books, 1993.

Williams, Virginia, and Redford Williams. *Lifeskills.* New York: Times Books, 1997.

HEALING OURSELVES TO HEAL SOCIETY

Achterberg, Jeanne. *Imagery and Healing: Shamanism and Modern Medicine.* Boston: New Science Library, 1985.

Achterberg, Jeanne. *Woman as Healer.* Boston: Shambhala, 1990.

Achterberg, Jeanne, Barbara Dossey, and Leslie Kolkmeier. *Rituals of Healing: Using Imagery for Health and Wellness.* New York: Bantam, 1994.

Barasch, Marc Ian. *The Healing Path.* New York: Tarcher/Putnam, 1993.

Benson, Herbert, with Mark Stark. *Timeless Healing: The Power and Biology of Belief.* New York: Scribner's, 1996.

Benson, Herbert, Eileen M. Stuart, and associates at the Mind/Body Medical Institute of the New England Deaconess Hospital and Harvard Medical School. *The Wellness Book: The Comprehensive Guide to Maintaining Health and Treating Stress-related Illness.* New York: Simon & Schuster, 1993.

Bolen, Jean Shinoda. *Close to the Bone: Life-threatening Illness and the Search For Meaning.* New York: Scribner, 1996.

Borysenko, Joan. *Fire in the Soul: A New Psychology of Spiritual Optimism.* New York: Warner, 1993.

Borysenko, Joan. *Minding the Body, Mending the Mind.* New York: Bantam, 1988.

Brigham, Deirdre Davis. *Imagery for Getting Well.* New York: Norton, 1994.

Chopra, Deepak. *Ageless Body, Timeless Mind: The Quantum Alternative to Growing Old.* New York: Harmony, 1993.

Chopra, Deepak. *Boundless Energy. The Complete Mind/Body Program for Overcoming Chronic Fatigue.* New York: Harmony, 1995.

Chopra, Deepak. *Journey into Healing: Awakening the Wisdom Within You.* New York: Harmony, 1994.

Cortis, Bruno. *Heart and Soul.* New York: Villard, 1995.

Cousins, Norman. *Anatomy of an Illness as Perceived by the Patient.* New York: Norton, 1979.

Curtis, Donald. *Your Thoughts Can Change Your Life.* New York: Warner, 1996.

Dienstfrey, Harris. *Where the Mind Meets the Body.* New York: HarperCollins, 1991.

Dossey, Larry. *Be Careful What You Pray For . . . You Just Might Get It.* San Francisco: HarperSanFrancisco, 1997.

Dossey, Larry. *Prayer Is Good Medicine.* San Francisco: HarperSanFrancisco, 1996.

Dreher, Henry. *The Immune Power Personality: 7 Traits You Can Develop to Stay Healthy.* New York: The Penguin Group, 1995.

Dunn, Rita, and Shirley A. Griggs. *Learning Styles and the Nursing Profession.* New York: National League of Nursing, 1998.

Goleman, Daniel, and Joel Gurin, eds. *Mind/Body Medicine: How to Use Your Mind for Better Health.* Yonkers: N.Y.: Consumer Reports Books, 1993.

Gordon, James. *Manifesto for a New Medicine: Your Guide to Healing Partnerships and the Wise Use of Alternative Therapies.* New York: Addison-Wesley, 1996.

Hirshberg, Caryle, and Mark Ian Barasch. *Remarkable Recovery: What Extraordinary Healings Tell Us About Getting Well and Staying Well.* New York: Riverhead, 1995.

Kabat-Zinn, Jon. *Full Catastrophe Living: Using the Wisdom of Your Body and Mind to Face Stress, Pain, and Illness.* New York: Delacorte Press, 1990.

Klaus, Rita. *Rita's Story.* Orleans, Mass.: Paraclete Press, 1994.

Knaster, Mirka. *Discovering the Body's Wisdom.* New York: Bantam, 1996.

Kübler-Ross, Elisabeth. *The Wheel of Life: A Memoir of Living and Dying.* New York: Scribner, 1997.

Kunz, Dora. *The Personal Aura.* Wheaton, Ill.: Quest, 1991.

Kreiger, Dolores. *Accepting Your Power to Heal: The Personal Practice of Therapeutic Touch.* Santa Fe, N.M.: Bear, 1993.

Kreiger, Dolores. *The Therapeutic Touch Inner Workbook: Ventures in Transpersonal Healing.* Santa Fe, N.M.: Bear, 1996.

Lerner, Michael. *Choices in Healing: Integrating the Best of Conventional and Complementary Approaches to Cancer.* Cambridge, Mass.: MIT Press, 1994.

Locke, Steven, and Douglas Colligan. *The Healer Within: The New Medicine of Mind and Body.* New York: Dutton, 1986.

Macrae, Janet. *Therapeutic Touch: A Practical Guide.* New York: Alfred Knopf, 1990.

The Medical Advisor: The Complete Guide to Alternative and Conventional Treatments. New York: Time-Life Books, 1996.

Mann, Ronald L. *Sacred Healing: Integrating Spirituality with Psychotherapy.* Nevada City, Calif.: Blue Dolphin, 1998.

Morton, Mary, and Michael Morton. *Five Steps to Selecting the Best Alternative Medicine: A Complete Guide to Complementary and Integrative Medicine.* Novato, Calif.: New World Library, 1996.

Moyers, Bill. *Healing and the Mind.* New York: Doubleday, 1993.

Murphy, Michael. *The Future of the Body: Explorations into the Further Evolution of Human Nature.* Los Angeles: Tarcher, 1992.

Myss, Caroline. *Anatomy of the Spirit: The Seven Stages of Power and Healing.* New York: Harmony, 1996.

Myss, Caroline. *Why People Don't Heal and How They Can.* New York: Harmony, 1997.

Northrup, Christiane. *Women's Bodies, Women's Wisdom: Creating Physical and Emotional Health and Healing.* New York: Bantam, 1994, 1998.

Ornish, Dean. *Dr. Dean Ornish's Program for Reversing Heart Disease.* New York: Random House, 1990.

Ornish, Dean. *Love & Survival: The Scientific Basis for the Healing Power of Intimacy.* New York: HarperCollins, 1998.

Ornish, Dean, with Janet Fletcher. *Everyday Cooking with Dr. Dean*

Ornish: 150 Easy, Low-fat, High-flavor Recipes. New York: HarperCollins, 1996.

Ornstein, Robert, and David Sobel. *The Healing Brain*. New York: Simon & Schuster, 1987.

Robbins, John. *Reclaiming Our Health: Exploding the Medical Myth and Embracing the Source of True Healing*. Tiburon, Calif.: H.J. Kramer, 1996.

Stratton, Elizabeth K. *Touching Spirit: A Journey of Healing and Personal Resurrection*. New York: Simon & Schuster, 1996.

Pelletier, Kenneth. *Sound Mind, Sound Body*. New York: Simon & Schuster, 1994.

Pert, Candace. *Molecules of Emotion: Why We Feel the Way We Feel*. New York: Scribner, 1997.

Remen, Rachel Naomi. *Kitchen Table Wisdom: Stories that Heal*. New York: Riverhead Books, 1996.

Rinpoche, Sogyal. *The Tibetan Book of Living and Dying*. San Francisco: HarperSanFrancisco, 1992.

Rossman, Martin. *Healing Yourself: A Step-by-Step Program for Better Health through Imagery*. New York: Pocket Books, 1990.

Siegel, Bernie. *How to Live Between Office Visits: A Guide to Life, Love and Health*. New York: HarperCollins, 1993.

Siegel, Bernie. *Love, Medicine, and Miracles*. San Francisco: Harper and Row, 1986.

Seligman, Martin E.P. *Learned Optimism: How to Change Your Mind and Your Life*. New York: Simon & Schuster, 1990.

Simonton, Carl O., and Reid Henson. *The Healing Journey*. New York: Bantam, 1994.

Simonton, Carl O., Stephanie Matthews-Simonton, and James Creighton. *Getting Well Again*. New York: Bantam, 1981.

Targ, Russell and Jane Katra. *Miracles of Mind: Exploring Nonlocal Consciousness and Spiritual Healing*. Novato, Calif.: New World Library, 1998.

Temoshok, Lydia, and Henry Dreher. *The Type C Connection: The Behavioral Links to Cancer and Your Health*. New York: Random House, 1992.

Thondup, Tulku. *The Healing Power of Mind: Simple Meditation Exercises for Health, Well-Being, and Enlightenment*. Boston: Shambhala, 1996.

Vaughan, Frances. *The Inward Arc: Healing in Psychotherapy and Spirituality*. Grass Valley, Calif.: Blue Dolphin, 1995.

Warter, Carlos. *Who Do You Think You Are?: The Healing Power of Your Sacred Self*. New York: Bantam Books, 1998.

Weil, Andrew. *Natural Health, Natural Medicine: A Comprehensive Manual for Wellness and Self-Care*. New York: Houghton Mifflin, 1995.

Weil, Andrew. *Spontaneous Healing: How to Discover and Enhance Your Body's Natural Ability to Maintain and Heal Itself*. New York: Knopf, 1995.

WORKING TO BENEFIT SOCIETY

Allen, Marc. *Visionary Business. An Entrepreneur's Guide to Success*. Novato, Calif.: New World Library, 1996.

Anderson, Nancy. *Work with Passion: How to Do What You Love for a Living*. Novato, Calif.: New World Library, 1995.

Autry, James A. *Confessions of an Accidental Businessman: It Takes a Lifetime to Find Wisdom*. San Francisco: Berrett-Koehler, 1996.

Autry, James A. *Life and Work*. New York: William Morrow, 1994.

Brandt, Barbara. *Whole Life Economics: Revaluing Daily Life*. Philadelphia: New Society Publishers, 1995.

Breton, Denise, and Christopher Largent. *The Soul of Economics: Spiritual Evolution Goes to the Marketplace*. Wilmington, Del.: Idea House, 1991.

Briskin, Alan. *The Stirring of Soul in the Workplace*. San Francisco: Berrett-Koehler, 1998.

Campbell, Susan. *From Chaos to Confidence: Survival Strategies for the New Workplace*. New York: Simon & Schuster, 1995.

Celente, Gerald. *Trends 2000: How to Prepare for and Profit from the Changes of the 21st Century*. New York: Warner, 1997.

Chappell, Tom. *The Soul of a Business: Managing for Profit and the Common Good*. New York: Bantam, 1993.

Covey, Stephen. *Principle-Centered Leadership*. New York: Simon & Schuster, 1992.

Daly, Herman E., and John B. Cobb. *For the Common Good: Redirecting the Economy toward Community, the Environment, and a Sustainable Future*. Boston: Beacon Press, 1989.

Daly, Herman. *Beyond Growth: The Economics of Sustainable Development*. Boston: Beacon Press, 1996.

Dominguez, Joe, and Vicki Robin. *Your Money or Your Life: Transforming Your Relationship with Money and Achieving Financial Independence*. New York: Viking Penguin, 1992.

Ekins, Paul, Mayer Hillman, and Robert Hutchinson. *The Gaia Atlas of Green Economics*. New York: Doubleday, 1992.

Elgin, Duane. *Voluntary Simplicity: Toward a Way of Life That Is Outwardly Simple, Inwardly Rich*. New York: Quill, 1993.

Ferber, Marianne A., and Julie A. Nelson, eds. *Beyond Economic Man: Feminist Theory and Economics*. Chicago: University of Chicago Press, 1993.

Fritz, Robert. *Corporate Tides: The Inescapable Laws of Organizational Structure*. San Francisco: Berrett-Koehler, 1996.

Fox, Matthew. *Reinvention of Work: A New Vision of Livelihood for Our Time*. San Francisco: HarperSanFrancisco, 1995.

Gilley, Kay. *Leading from the Heart: Choosing Courage over Fear in the Workplace*. Boston: Butterworth-Heinemann, 1997.

Green, Alan. *A Company Discovers Its Soul*. San Francisco: Berrett-Koehler, 1996.

Green, Gareth, and Frank Baker. *Work, Health, and Productivity*. New York: Oxford University Press, 1991.

Harman, Willis, and John Hormann. *Creative Work: The Constructive Role of Business in Transforming Society*. Indianapolis: Knowledge Systems, 1990.

Hawken, Paul. *The Ecology of Commerce: A Declaration of Sustainability*. New York: HarperCollins, 1993.

Henderson, Hazel. *Building a Win-Win World: Life Beyond Global Economic Warfare*. San Francisco: Berrett-Koehler, 1996.

Hillman, James. *Kinds of Power: A Guide to Its Intelligent Uses.* New York: Currency/Doubleday, 1995.

Jarow, Rick. *Creating the Work You Love: Courage, Commitment, and Career.* Vermont: Destiny Books, 1995.

Korten, David. *When Corporations Rule the World.* San Francisco: Berrett-Koehler, 1995.

Makhijani, Arjun. *From Global Capitalism to Economic Justice: An Inquiry into the Elimination of System Poverty, Violence, and Environmental Destruction in the World Economy.* New York: Apex Press, 1992.

Meeker-Lowry, Susan. *Invested in the Common Good: Economics as if the Earth Really Mattered.* Philadelphia: New Society, 1995.

Naisbitt, Hohn, and Patricia Aburden. *Re-inventing the Corporation.* New York: Warner Books, 1985.

Needleman, Jacob. *Money and the Meaning of Life.* New York: Doubleday, 1991.

Peters, Thomas, and Robert Waterman, Jr. *In Search of Excellence.* New York: Warner, 1984.

Ray, Michael, and Alan Rinzler, eds. *The New Paradigm in Business: Emerging Strategies for Leadership and Organizational Change.* New York: Tarcher/Perigree, 1993.

Renesch, John, and Bill DeFoore, eds. *The New Bottom Line: Bringing Heart and Soul to Business.* San Francisco: New Leaders, 1996.

Rifkin, Jeremy. *The End of Work: The Decline of the Global Labor Force and the Dawn of the Post-Market Era.* New York: Tarcher/Putnam, 1995.

Roddick, Anita. *Body and Soul: Profits with Principles.* New York: Crown, 1991.

Schor, Juliet B. *The Overworked American: The Unexpected Decline of Leisure.* New York: Basic Books, 1993.

Schumacher, E.F. *Small Is Beautiful: Economics as if People Mattered.* San Francisco: Harper & Row, 1973.

Toms, Justine Willis, and Michael Toms. *True Work: The Sacred Dimension of Earning a Living.* New York: Bell Tower, 1998.

WHOLE WAYS TO LEARN

Armstrong, Thomas. *Seven Kinds of Smart: Identifying and Developing Your Many Intelligences.* New York: Plume/Penguin, 1993.

Botkin, James, Mahdi Elmandjra, and Malitza Mircea. *No Limits to Learning.* Elmsford, N.Y.: Pergamon Press, 1987.

Campbell, Bruce, and Linda Campell, and Dee Dickinson. *Teaching and Learning Through Multiple Intelligences.* New York: Allyn & Bacon, 1996.

Clark, Barbara. *Growing Up Gifted: Developing the Potential of Children at Home and at School.* Columbus, Ohio: Merrill Publishing, 1997.

Collins, Cathy, and John M. Mangieri, eds. *Teaching Thinking: An Agenda for the 21st Century.* New Jersey: Lawrence Erlbaum and Associates, 1992.

Crowell, Sam, Renate N. Caine, and Geoffrey Caine. *The Re-Enchantment of Learning: A Manual for Teacher Renewal and Classroom Transformation.* Tucson, Ariz.: Zephyr Press, 1998.

Csikszentmihalyi, Mihaly. *Flow: The Psychology of Optimal Experience.* New York: Harper and Row, 1990.

Diamond, Marian. *Magic Trees of the Mind: How to Nurture Your Child's Intelligence, Creativity, and Healthy Emotions from Birth to Adolescence.* New York: Dutton, 1998.

Dunn, Rita, Kenneth Dunn, and Janet Perrin. *Teaching Young Children Through Their Individual Learning Styles: Personal Approaches for Grades K-12.* Boston: Allyn and Bacon, 1993.

Dunn, Rita, and Shirley Griggs. *Multi-Culturalism and Learning Style: Teaching and Counseling Adolescents.* Westport, Conn.: Praeger, 1995.

Gardner, Howard. *Frames of Mind: The Theory of Multiple Intelligences.* New York: Basic Books, 1993.

Gardner, Howard. *Multiple Intelligences: The Theory in Practice.* New York: Basic Books, 1993.

Goleman, Daniel. *Emotional Intelligence: Why It Can Matter More Than IQ.* New York: Bantam Books, 1997.

Goodlad, John. *Places Where Teachers Are Taught.* San Francisco: Jossey-Bass, 1990.

Healy, Jane. *Endangered Minds: Why Our Children Don't Think and What We Can Do About It.* New York: Simon and Schuster, 1991.

Kilpatrick, William. *Why Johnny Can't Tell Right from Wrong.* New York: Simon & Schuster, 1993.

Lantieri, Linda, and Janet Patti. *Waging Peace in Our Schools.* Boston: Beacon Press, 1996.

Lickona, Thomas. *Educating for Character: How Our Schools Can Teach Respect and Responsibility.* New York: Bantam, 1992.

Maclean, Paul D. *The Triune Brain in Evolution.* New York and London: Plenum Press, 1995.

Noddings, Nel. *The Challenge to Care in Schools.* New York: Teachers College Press, Columbia University, 1992.

Palmer, Parker J. *The Courage to Teach: Exploring the Inner Landscape of a Teacher's Life.* San Francisco: Jossey-Bass Publishers, 1998.

Perkins, David. *Smart Schools: From Training Memories to Educating Minds.* New York: The Free Press, 1995.

Sergiovanni, Thomas J. *Moral Leadership.* San Francisco: Jossey-Bass Publishers, 1996.

Sizer, Theodore. *Horace's School: Redesigning the American High School.* New York: Houghton Mifflin, 1993.

Sternberg, Robert. *Beyond IQ: A Triarchic Theory of Human Intelligence.* New York: Cambridge University Press, 1984.

Wynne, Edward A., and Kevin Ryan. *Reclaiming Our Schools: Teaching Character Academics and Discipline.* New York: Macmillan, 1996.

THE ENVIRONMENTAL CONNECTION

Augros, Robert, and George Stanciu. *The New Biology: Discovering the Wisdom in Nature.* Boston and London: New Science Library, Shambhala, 1987.

Berry, Thomas. *Dream of the Earth.* San Francisco: Sierra Club Books, 1988.

Berry, Wendell. *The Unsettling of America: Culture and Agriculture.* San Francisco: Sierra Club Books, 1996.

Brower, David. *Let the Mountains Talk, Let the Rivers Run: A Call to Those Who Would Save the Earth.* San Francisco: CollinsWest, 1995.

Devall, Bill. *Simple in Means, Rich in Ends: Practicing Deep Ecology.* Salt Lake City, Utah: Peregrine Smith Books, 1988.

De Waal, Frans B.M. *Good Natured: The Origins of Right and Wrong in Human and Other Animals.* Cambridge, Mass.: Harvard University Press, 1996.

The EarthWorks Group. *50 Simple Things You Can Do to Save The Earth.* Berkeley, Calif.: Earthworks Press, 1989.

Elgin, Duane. *Awakening Earth: Exploring the Evolution of Human Culture and Consciousness.* New York: Morrow, 1993.

Elgin, Duane. *Voluntary Simplicity.* New York: Morrow, 1993.

Ehrlich, Paul R., and Anne H. Ehrlich. *Betrayal of Science and Reason: How Anti-Environmental Rhetoric Threatens Our Future.* Washington, D.C: Island Press, 1996.

Ehrlich, Paul R., and Anne H. Ehrlich. *The Population Explosion.* New York: Simon & Schuster, 1990.

Ehrlich, Paul R., Anne H. Ehrlich, and Gretchen D. Daily. *The Stork and the Plow: The Equity Answer to the Human Dilemma.* New York: Putnam, 1995.

Goodall, Jane. *With Love.* Silver Springs, Md.: The Jane Goodall Institute, 1994.

Hawken, Paul: *The Ecology of Commerce: A Declaration of Sustainability.* New York: HarperCollins, 1993.

Heinberg, Richard. *A New Covenant with Nature: Notes on the End of Civilization and the Renewal of Culture.* Wheaton, Ill.: Quest, 1996.

Jackson, Wes. *Becoming Native to This Place.* Lexington, Ky.: University Press of Kentucky, 1994.

Kolb, Janice Gray. *Compassion for All Creatures.* Nevada City, Calif.: Blue Dolphin, 1997.

Lerner, Steve. *Eco-Pioneers: Practical Visionaries Solving Today's Environmental Problems.* Cambridge, Mass.: MIT Press, 1997.

Mander, Jerry. *In the Absence of the Sacred: The Failure of Technology & the Survival of the Indian Nations.* San Francisco: Sierra Club Books, 1991.

McKibben, Bill. *Hope, Human and Wild: True Stories of Living Lightly on the Earth.* New York: Little Brown, 1995.

Meadows, Donella H., Dennis Meadows, and Jørgen Randers. *Beyond the Limits: Confronting Global Collapse, Envisioning a Sustainable Future.* White River Junction, Vt.: Chelsea Green Publishing, 1992.

Mills, Stephanie. *In Service of the Wild: Restoring and Reinhabiting Damaged Land.* Boston: Beacon Press, 1995.

Oelschlaeger, Max. *The Idea of Wilderness.* New Haven & London: Yale University Press, 1991.

Roszak, Theodore. *The Voice of the Earth.* New York: Simon & Schuster, 1992.

Sessions, George, ed. *Deep Ecology for the 21st Century: Readings on the Philosophy and Practice of the New Environmentalism.* Boston: Shambhala, 1995.

Snyder, Gary. *The Practice of the Wild.* Berkeley, Calif.: North Point Press, 1990.

LIVING AS A WORK OF ART

Allen, Pat B. *Art Is a Way of Knowing: A Guide to Self-Knowledge and Spiritual Fulfillment Through Creating.* Boston: Shambhala, 1995.

Albert, Susan Wittig. *Writing from Life: Telling Your Soul's Story.* New York: Tarcher/Putnam, 1996.

Bonny, Helen L., and Louis M. Savary. *Music and Your Mind: Listening with a New Consciousness.* New York: Station Hill Press, 1990.

Boxill, Edith Hillman. *Music Therapy for Living.* St. Louis, Mo.: MMB Music, 1989.

Bryan, Mark, with Julia Cameron, and Catherine Allen. *The Artist's Way at Work.* New Jersey: William Morrow, 1998.

Cameron, Julia. *The Artist's Way: A Spiritual Path to Higher Creativity.* New York: Tarcher/Putnam, 1992.

Cameron, Julia. *The Vein of Gold: A Journey to Your Creative Heart.* New York: Tarcher/Putnam, 1996.

Campbell, Don. *Music and Miracles.* Wheaton, Ill.: Quest, 1992.

Campbell, Don. *Music, Physician for Times to Come: An Anthology.* Wheaton Ill.: Quest, 1991.

Cornell, Judith. *Mandala: Luminous Symbols for Healing.* Wheaton Ill.: Quest Books, 1994.

Foehr, Regina Paxton, and Susan A. Schiller, eds. *The Spiritual Side of Writing: Releasing the Learner's Whole Potential.* Portsmouth, N.H.: Boynton/Cook Publishers, 1997.

Goleman, Daniel, Paul Kaufman, and Michael Ray. *The Creative Spirit.* New York: Dutton, 1992.

Halprin, Anna. *Moving Toward Life: Five Decades of Transformational Dance.* Hanover & London: Wesleyan University Press, 1995.

Huang, Chungliang A., and Jerry Lynch. *Thinking Body, Dancing Mind.* New York: Bantam, 1992.

Maisel, Eric. *Fearless Creating: A Step-by-Step Guide to Starting and Completing Your Work of Art.* New York: Tarcher/Putnam, 1995.

Mathieu, W.A. *The Listening Book.* Boston: Shambhala, 1991.

Phillips, Jan. *Marry Your Muse: Making a Lasting Commitment to Your Creativity.* Wheaton, Ill.: Quest Books, 1997.

Sacks, Oliver. *Awakenings.* New York: HarperCollins, 1990

Samuels, Michael, & Mary Rockwood Lane. *Creative Healing: How to Heal Yourself by Tapping Your Inner Creativity.* San Francisco: HarperSanFrancisco, 1998.

Sewell, Marilyn, ed. *Claiming the Spirit Within: A Sourcebook of Women's Poetry.* Boston: Beacon Press, 1996.

Wakefield, Dan. *Creating from the Spirit: Living Each Day as a Creative Act.* New York: Ballantine Books, 1996.

The following resource guide lists the organizations mentioned in this book, as well as other groups and networks. This is by no means a definitive list. It is, rather, a sample of the organizations actively working to improve society. Even so, a glance at these grassroots socially active organizations is inspiring. Across the country, people are volunteering their time to work for causes and issues they care about. Most of the groups listed in this guide are nonprofit; their efforts usually receive little publicity or recognition and it takes dedication and commitment to keep them afloat. However, if you become pessimistic about our society's problems, reflect upon the millions of individuals who are finding ways to work for a better future. Thank them. Join them. Support them.

HOLISTIC ORGANIZATIONS

Action Coalition for Global Change
55 New Montgomery St., Suite 219
San Francisco, CA 94105
Tel: (415) 896-2242
Fax: (415) 227-4878
E-mail: acgc@igc.apc.org
Website: http://idaho-web.com

Membership group of over sixty nongovernmental agencies. This coalition has formed a global network to promote peace, a just global economy, a healthy environment, and human rights for all.

America's Promise — The Alliance for Youth
909 N. Washington St., Suite 400
Alexandria, VA 22314
Tel: (703) 684-4500
Fax: (703) 684-7328
Website: http://www.americaspromise.org

Retired General Colin Powell is chairman of America's Promise, an organization formed to improve the lives of the nation's more than 15 million at-risk youth. They serve as a nationwide catalyst — urging public, private, and nonprofit organizations to make the most of their combined talents and resources to help young people lead happy, healthy, and productive lives.

Angeles Arrien Foundation for
Cross-Cultural Education and Research
P.O. Box 1278
Sausalito, CA 94966
Tel: (415) 331-1890
Fax: (415) 331-5069

This group's purpose is to integrate the wisdom of indigenous peoples into contemporary culture by honoring their oral traditions, arts, myths, and deep respect for nature. The foundation introduces activities that enhance creativity and creative problem solving, develop communication and leadership skills from a cross-cultural perspective, and explore community building and multicultural conflict resolution.

The Association of World Citizens
55 New Montgomery St., Suite 224
San Francisco, CA 94105
Tel: (415) 541-9610
E-mail: worldcit@best.com
Website: http://www.worldcitizens.org

An international peace and justice organization with branches in fifty countries, and NGO status with the United Nations. Their goal is to convince people to think and act as citizens of the world, and help build a global village of lasting peace, social and economic justice, and a sustainable environment for future generations.

The California Institute of Integral Studies
9 Peter Yorke Way
San Francisco, CA 94109
Tel: (415) 674-5500
Fax: (415) 674-5555
E-mail: info@ciis.edu
Website: http://www.ciis.edu

International institute of higher learning offering courses that embody spirit, intellect, and wisdom.

Center for Citizen Initiatives
Presidio Bldg. 1008, 1st flr., Thoreau Ctr.
P.O. Box 29912
San Francisco, CA 94129-0912
Tel: (415) 561-7777
Fax: (415) 561-7778
E-mail: cci@igc.org
Website: http://www.igc.org/cci/

This center emerged as a pioneer in diplomacy between the United States and the former Soviet Union in the '80s. CCI closely monitors the rapid changes taking place in the newly independent states and responds with programs targeted at citizens' needs.

Center for Partnership Studies
P.O. Box 51936
Pacific Grove, CA 93950

Tel: (408) 626-1004
Fax: (408) 626-3734
Website: http://www.partnershipway.org
Based on Riane Eisler's research, the center's goal is to develop opportunities for men and women to live in partnership in all parts of the globe, and foster equitable relationships — whether intimate or international.

Changing Systems
P.O. Box 695
Larkspur, CA 94977
Tel: (415) 924-7347
E-mail: ccs@igc.org
An educational organization that teaches a new open-systems model of human communication and cooperation. Their programs teach a set of skills and strategies for cooperation at every level of human experience.

Children of the Earth, Inc.
Heart's Bend World Children's Center
P.O. Box 217
Newfane, VT 05345
Tel: (802) 365-7797
Fax: (802) 365-7798
E-mail: coevt@aol.com
Children of the Earth, an official United Nations NGO, supports children in creating new social models that embody their understanding of the interconnectedness of all life, and the need to consciously sustain life on our planet. Young people participate in international leadership programs to prepare for their role as world citizens and future leaders.

Children: Our Ultimate Investment
P.O. Box 1868
Los Angeles, CA 90028
Tel: (213) 461-8248
Fax: (213) 461-8470
Founded by Laura Huxley, this organization informs and educates the public on scientific research and humanistic ideals relating to the preparation for conception, pregnancy, birth, and the first five years of life.

Coalition for Healthier Cities and Communities
c/o Health Research and Educational Trust
One North Franklin
Chicago, IL 60606
Tel: (312) 422-2635
Fax: (312) 422-4568
E-mail: healthy@aha.org
Website: http://www.healthycommunities.org
The coalition is a growing network of 450 community partnerships, organizations, and individuals representing health care providers, human service agencies, public health departments, community advocacy groups, businesses, academic and religious institutions, and federal and local governments — all collaborating to focus attention and resources on improving the health and quality of life of communities. Its website provides a database of community contacts, resources, and discussion forums to facilitate direct collaboration between communities.

Cultural Environment Movement
P.O. Box 31847
Philadelphia, PA 19104
Tel: (215) 204-6434
Fax: (215) 204-5823
E-Mail: cem@libertynet.org
Website: http://www/cemnet.org
International coalition of organizations united in working for freedom, fairness, gender equity, diversity, and democratic decision making.

Delancey Street Foundation
600 Embarcadero St.
San Francisco, CA 94107
Tel: (415) 957-9800
Foundation founded by Mimi Silbert. Their rehabilitation program provides housing, training skills, and work for ex-convicts and people with drug and alcohol problems — transforming society's outcasts into responsible citizens. Programs are based in San Francisco, New York, North Carolina, New Mexico, and Los Angeles.

Do Something
423 W. 55th St., 8th Floor
New York, NY 10022
Tel: (212) 523-1175
Fax: (212) 582-1307
Website: http://www.dosomething.org

Do Something works to inspire young people to believe that change is possible. They train, fund, and mobilize them to be leaders; their vision is that young people will take direct action to strengthen their communities.

Esalen Institute
Highway One
Big Sur, CA 93920-9616
Tel: (408) 667-3000
Fax: (408) 667-2724
Website: http://www.esalen.org

This center "explores work in the humanities and sciences that promotes human values and potentials." Esalen offers public seminars, residential work-study programs, and invitational conferences.

Fetzer Institute
9292 West KL Ave.
Kalamazoo, MI 49009
Tel: (616) 375-2000
Fax: (616) 372-2163
Website: http://www.fetzer.org

Private foundation dedicated to initiating partnerships for the purpose of research, education, and service in mind-body-spirit health and healing.

Foundation for Conscious Evolution
P.O. Box 6397
San Rafael, CA 94903-0397
Tel: (415) 454-8191
Fax: (415) 454-8805
E-mail: fce@peaceroom.org
Website: http://www.cocreation.org

Organization founded by Barbara Marx Hubbard as a point of orientation and communication for ideas and projects that are now co-creating a positive and life-enhancing world. The Cocreation website is designed to scan for breakthroughs, successes, and models that work in every major sector of human endeavor.

Foundation for Ethics and Meaning
26 Fell St.
San Francisco, CA 94102
Tel: (415) 552-6336
Fax: (415) 575-1434
Website: http://members.aol.com/pomeaning
Michael Lerner began this national movement for a "politics of meaning." The foundation organizes annual conferences, study groups, and develops policies to show how a society might work if based on caring, meaning, and spiritual sensitivity.

Foundation for Global Community
222 High St.
Palo Alto, CA 94301
Tel: (650) 328-7756
Fax: (650) 328-7785
E-mail: info@globalcommunity.org
Website: http://www.globalcommunity.org
An educational organization with the mission "to discover, live, and communicate what is needed to build a world that functions for the benefit of all life." Publishes *Timeline*, a bimonthly magazine.

The Giraffe Project
P.O. Box 759
Langley, WA 98260
Tel: (360) 221-7989
Fax: (360) 221-7817
E-mail: office@giraffe.org
Website: http://www.giraffe.org/giraffe/
This project recognizes people who stick their necks out for the common good. Organizes workshops and seminars to inspire businesses and organizations to adopt the "Giraffe Spirit." See Education Chapter Resources for the Giraffe curriculum guide.

Global Education Associates
475 Riverside Dr., Suite 1848
New York, NY 10115
Tel: (212) 870-3290
Fax: (212) 870-2729
E-mail: gea475@igc.apc.org.
Website: http://www.igc.apc.org/gea

A network of men and women in over ninety countries committed to promoting global systems that advance a more just and peaceful world order.

Global Exchange
2017 Mission St., Room 303
San Francisco, CA 94110
Tel: (415) 255-7296
Fax: (415) 255-7498
E-mail: gx-info@globalexchange.org
Website: http://www.globalexchange.org

Global Exchange is an education and advocacy organization dedicated to linking North Americans with grassroots groups working for social justice, human rights, and sustainable development around the world. They are specifically involved in campaigns to influence policy, and human rights action programs. They also operate stores that give fair profits back to developing world artisans.

The Hunger Project
15 East 26th St., Suite 1401
New York, NY 10010
Tel: (212) 251-9100
Fax: (212) 532-9785
E-mail: info@thp.org
Website: http://www.thp.org.thp

The Hunger Project empowers people to discover their vision, express their leadership, and work together to solve hunger's root causes.

Institute for Food and Development Policy — Food First
398 60th St.
Oakland, CA 94618

Tel: (510) 654-4400
Fax: (510) 654-4551
E-mail: foodfirst@igc.apc.org
Website: http://www.foodfirst.org
This institute addresses the root causes of hunger, poverty, and environmental decline.

Institute of Noetic Sciences
475 Gate Five Rd., Suite 300
Sausalito, CA 94965
Tel: (415) 331-5650
Fax: (415) 331-5673
Website: http://www.noetic.org
Research foundation, educational institution, and membership organization, with over 50,000 members worldwide. They provide seed grants for leading-edge scientific and scholarly research to study the mind and its diverse ways of knowing in a rigorous and truly interdisciplinary fashion. Members are invited to participate in local community groups, lectures, annual conferences, and travel programs. Through these activities the institute hopes to create a humane, sustainable, and peaceful world. Publishes *Noetic Sciences Review* and *Connections*.

International Healthy Cities Foundation
c/o Dr. Leonard Duhl
Public Health Institute
2001 Addison St.
Berkeley, CA 94704-1103
Tel: (510) 642-1715
Fax: (510) 643-6981
E-mail: hcities@uclink2.berkeley.edu
Website: http://www.healthycities.org
This foundation focuses on the total quality of life in cities and communities, showing concern for the physical infrastructure (land, water, air, waste, transport, and communication technology) as well as the social infrastructure (culture, relationships, networks of support, governance, education, and participation). In cities throughout the world, they urge cooperative action among individuals and groups in government, social

services, businesses, and education to encourage people to work together. Their approach is to resolve problems by viewing each city as an ecological whole system. They are particularly concerned about the total health of children, and have created local coalitions to explore children's issues.

Millennium Institute

1117 North 19th St., Suite 900
Arlington, VA 22209-1708
Tel: (703) 841-0048
Fax: (703) 841-0050
E-mail: millennium@igc.apc.org.
Website: http://www.igc.apc.org/millennium

The Millennium Institute promotes long-term, integrated global thinking by sponsoring programs, publications, research, and training. They integrate what is known about trends affecting Earth with practical actions that can make a vital difference.

Mount Madonna Center

445 Summit Rd.
Watsonville, CA 95076
Tel: (408) 847-0406
Fax: (408) 847-2683
E-mail: programs@mountmadonna.org
Website: http://www.mountmadonna.org

Retreat and conference facility, as well as spiritual community. Programs in yoga and related disciplines. Facilities available to outside groups of up to 500.

Namasté Retreat & Conference Center

at Living Enrichment Center
29500 S.W. Grahams Ferry Rd.
Wilsonville, OR 97070-9516
Tel: (800) 893-1000
Website: http://www.lecworld.org

Located in the woods of the Pacific Northwest, this center serves people on a spiritual quest — learning, living, and serving.

New Civilization Network
Website: http://www.worldtrans.org
This website explores emerging possibilities for a better quality of life on our planet.

New York Open Center
83 Spring St.
New York, NY 10012
Tel: (212) 219-2527
Fax: (212) 219-1347
E-mail: nyocreg@aol.com
Website: http://www.opencenter.org
One of the largest holistic learning centers in the United States, offering classes, lectures, and retreats, and acting as a clearinghouse for holistic ideas in health, religion, the environment, and the arts. Publishes the magazine *Lapis: The Inner Meaning of Contemporary Life* three times a year.

Omega Institute for Holistic Studies
260 Lake Dr.
Rhinebeck, NY 12572
Tel: (914) 266-4444 or (800) 944-1001
Website: http://www.omega-inst.org
The country's largest alternative education and retreat center's lakeside campus offers more than 250 workshops on holistic health, psychological inquiry, world music and art, meditation, and new forms of spiritual practice.

Pathways to Peace
P.O. Box 1057
Larkspur, CA 94977
Tel: (415) 461-0500
Fax: (415) 925-0330
E-mail: pathways@worldpeace.org
Website: http://pathwaystopeace.org
An international peacebuilding, educational, and consulting organization. Their mission is to expand the comprehension and expression of peace

and peacebuilding practices at all levels, and to build cooperation by uniting and enhancing the strengths of existing organizations and programs.

Ploughshares Fund
Fort Mason Center
San Francisco, CA 94123
Tel: (415) 775-2244
Fax: (415) 775-4529
E-mail: ploughshares@igc.apc.org
Website: http://www.ploughshares.org

Public and grant-making foundation, founded by Sally Lilienthal, with the purpose of building "global security in the nuclear age."

Points of Light Foundation
1400 I St., N.W., Suite 800
Washington, D.C. 2005-2208
Tel: (202) 729-8000
E-mail: volnet.aol.com
Website: http://www.pointsoflight.org

The mission of this nonpartisan foundation is "to engage more people more effectively in volunteer community service to help solve serious social problems." The Foundation provides products, training, consultation, publications, and technical assistance materials through a network of over 500 volunteer centers and partnerships with corporations, nonprofits, and individuals. To increase interest in volunteering they sponsor various awards and also promote national service events, such as the National Youth Service Day.

Positive Futures Network
P.O. Box 10818
Bainbridge Island, WA 98110-0818
Tel: (206) 842-0216
Fax: (206) 842-5208
E-mail: yes@futurenet.org
Website: http://www.futurenet.org

This network explores positive new developments in a wide variety of areas, tracking an emerging, more compassionate culture. Publishes *Yes! A Journal of Positive Futures.*

Right Livelihood Award Foundation
P.O. Box 15072
S-10465 Stockholm, Sweden
Tel: (08) 7020340
Fax: (08) 7020338
International code +46
E-mail: info@rightlivelihood.se
Presents annual Right Livelihood Awards to honor pioneers in economics, health, peace, and development. Their purpose is to stimulate a debate about the values underlying society, and to stress a holistic approach to today's challenges.

Rocky Mountain Institute
1739 Snowmass Creek Rd.
Snowmass, CO 81654-9199
Tel: (970) 927-3851
Fax: (970) 927-4178
E-Mail: outreach@rmi.org
Website: http://www.rmi.org
Independent research and educational foundation founded by Amory and Hunter Lovins. Their mission is to foster the efficient and sustainable use of resources to further global security.

Search for Common Ground
1601 Connecticut Ave., N.W., Suite 200
Washington, D.C. 20009
Tel: (202) 265-4300
Fax: (202) 232-6718
E-mail: scmarks@sfcg.org
Website: http://www.sfcg.org
An international nongovernmental organization that pursues new ways of thinking about conflicts and new approaches to find cooperative solutions.

Social Innovations in Global Management (SIGMA)
Department of Organizational Behavior
Weatherhead School of Management
Case Western Reserve University
Cleveland, OH 44106

Tel: (216) 368-2215
Fax: (216) 368-4785
E-mail: bjr3@po.cwru.edu
Website: http://weatherhead.cwru.edu/gem

SIGMA is a program of research and education at the Weatherhead School of Management dedicated to the development of worldwide organizations capable of addressing complex global issues. SIGMA concentrates its efforts on the new and most promising forms of organization and management that make possible human cooperation in the service of global sustainability and well-being. It accomplishes its mission through research, management education, and related activities.

State of the World Forum

The Presidio
P.O. Box 29434
San Francisco, CA 94129
Tel: (415) 561-2345
Fax: (415) 561-2323
E-mail: forum@worldforum.org
Website: http://www.worldforum.org

An educational foundation with no political, economic, or partisan affiliation, the forum is a global network of individuals seeking solutions, with a multidisciplinary approach, to the challenges facing humanity in the twenty-first century.

The Windstar Foundation

2317 Snowmass Creek Rd.
Snowmass, CO 81654-9198
Tel: (970) 927-4777
Fax: (970) 927-4779
E-mail: windstar@rof.net
Website: http://www.wstar.org

See Education Resource Guide for students and educators. Environmental education organization founded by John Denver and Thomas Crum to inspire individuals to make responsible choices and take direct personal action to achieve a peaceful and sustainable future. Provides a networking base and on-site workshops

World Future Society
7910 Woodmont Ave., Suite 450
Bethesda, MD 20814
Tel: (301) 656-8274
Fax: (301) 951-0394
E-mail: wfsinfo@wfs.org
Website: http://www.wfs.org-wfs
Holds annual conferences and publishes a bi-monthly journal, *The Futurist*, which explores forecasts, trends, and ideas about the future.

CHAPTER ONE:
Building a Connection between Spirituality and Science

The Association for Global New Thought
1565 Maple Ave., Suite 204-205
Evanston, IL 60201
Tel: (847) 866-9525
E-mail: agnt2000@aol.com
Website: http://www.gandhiking.com
This association embodies and communicates a spiritual way of life honoring humankind's oneness, through principles and practices that nurture co-creation. Its initiatives promote the awareness of nonviolence and peacemaking as a way to heal, transform, and empower people and their communities.

The Center for Frontier Sciences
Temple University
Ritter Hall 478
Philadelphia, PA 19122
Tel: (215) 204-8487
Fax: (215) 204-5553
E-mail: v2058a@vm.temple.edu.
Website: http://www/temple.edu/cfs
Hosts lectures and conferences, and provides information on frontier issues of science, medicine, and technology. Publishes *Frontier Perspectives*, a semiannual journal that examines the frontier issues in science, medicine, and technology.

The Center for Science Within Consciousness
10801 Lagrima de Oro N.E., #813
Albuquerque, NM 87111
E-mail: hswift@swcp.com

A network that examines a spiritualized science, incorporating consciousness as a primary reality. Publishes biannual bulletin.

Center for Theology and the Natural Sciences
2400 Ridge Rd.
Berkeley, CA 94709
Tel: (510) 848-8152
Fax: (510) 848-2535
E-mail: ctns2gtu@ctns.org
Website: http://www.ctns.org

The mission of CTNS is to promote the creative mutual interaction between theology and the natural sciences; they pursue this goal through teaching, public service, and research. They offer accredited courses, and their Science and Spiritual Quest Project, sponsored by the Templeton Foundation, brings together physicists, cosmologists, biologists, and computer and information technology specialists.

Center for World Thanksgiving at Thanks-Giving Square
P.O. Box 1770
Dallas, TX 75221-1770
Tel: (214) 969-1977
Fax: (214) 754-0152
E-Mail: info@thanksgiving.org
Website: http://www.thanksgiving.org

An interfaith, multicultural educational organization, using thanksgiving and gratitude to build bridges between diverse peoples.

Council for a Parliament of the World's Religions
P.O. Box 1630
Chicago, IL 60690-1630
Tel: (312) 629-2990
Fax: (312) 629-2991
E-mail: spiritcpwr@aol.com

The first Parliament of World's Religion, held in conjunction with the World Columbian Exposition, took place in Chicago in 1893. CPWR is continuing the spirit and legacy of the Parliament by fostering interreligious dialogue and cooperation around the world.

Hunger Project (See address under Holistic Organizations.)

Institute on Religion and Public Life
156 5th Ave., Suite 400
New York, NY 10010
Tel: (212) 627-2288
Fax: (212) 627-2184
E-mail: rjn001.aol.com
Website: http://www.firstthings.com
Interrelgious, nonpartisan research and education institute.

Interfaith Center at the Presidio
2107 Van Ness Ave., Suite 300
San Francisco, CA 94109
Tel: (415) 775-4635
Fax: (415) 771-8681
Website: http://www.interfaith.presidio.org
The mission of the Interfaith Center is to welcome and celebrate the diverse spiritual wisdom of the faith traditions in the San Francisco Bay Area.

International Interfaith Centre
2 Market Street
Oxford OX1 3EF
United Kingdom
Tel: 44 (0)1865 202745
Fax: 44 (0)1865 202746
E-mail: iic@interfaith-center.org
Website: http://www.interfaith-center.org
The International Interfaith Centre (IIC) was founded in 1993 by the International Association for Religious Freedom, the World Congress of Faiths, and Westminster College, Oxford. It supports the interfaith work of organizations and individuals to further community building between people with different faiths, particularly those living

in situations of conflict. IIC initiates and facilitates cooperative programs and research to promote community renewal and reconciliation. It acts as a network link for international and national organizations involved in interfaith activities.

**International Society for the Study
of Subtle Energies & Energy Medicine**
356 Goldco Circle
Golden, CO 80403-1347
Tel: (303) 425-4625
Fax: (303) 425-4685
E-mail: 74040,1273@compuserve.com or issseem@compuserve.com
Website: http://vitalenergy.com/issseem/
Society concerned with the study of informational systems and energies that interact with the human psyche and physiology. Publishes *Bridges* magazine, directed toward health professionals and the general public, and *Subtle Energies and Energy Medicine*, a medical journal, published three times a year.

Millennium Institute (See address under Holistic Organizations.)

Society for Scientific Exploration
P.O. Box 5848
Stanford, CA 94309-5848
Tel: (650) 593-8581
Fax: (650) 595-4466
E-mail: sims@jse.com
Website: http://www.jse.com
Membership organization explores ideas and topics that challenge established scientific beliefs. Publishes *Journal of Scientific Exploration*, an international journal that offers a professional forum for the presentation, scrutiny, and criticism of scientific research on topics outside the established disciplines of science.

The Spiritual Emergence Network
930 Mission St., #7
Santa Cruz, CA 95060

Tel: (408) 426-0902
E-mail: sen@cruzio.com
Website: http://elfi.com/sen
International information and referral service, staffed by volunteers, to help people who are interested in, or are experiencing, nonordinary spiritual states.

John Templeton Foundation
Two Radnor Corporate Center
100 Matsonford Rd., Suite 320
Radnor, PA 19087
Tel: (610) 687-8942
Fax: (610) 687-8961
Website: http://www.templeton.org
The John Templeton Foundation was established in 1987 by renowned international investor Sir John Templeton to encourage progress in life's moral and spiritual dimensions. The foundation works closely with scientists, theologians, medical professionals, philosophers, and other scholars. The foundation currently funds more than 150 projects, studies, award programs, and publications worldwide. The Templeton Prize for Progress in Religion is awarded annually to an individual of any religious tradition or movement whose ideas or research contributes to our spiritual knowledge.

Union of Concerned Scientists
2 Brattle Square
Cambridge, MA 02238
Tel: (617) 547-5552
Fax: (617) 864-9405
E-mail: ucs@ucsusa.org
Website: http://www.ucsusa.org
National organization dedicated to advancing responsible public policies in areas where science and technology play a critical role. They are involved in arms control and international security issues, agriculture, biotechnology, and concerns about energy, transportation, global warning, and global resources.

The United Religions Initiative
P.O. Box 29242
Presidio Building, #1009, First floor
San Francisco, CA 94129-0242
Tel: (415) 561-2300
Fax: (415) 561-2313
E-mail: office@united-religions.org
Website: http://www.united-religions.org

The mission of the United Religions Initiative is to create the United Religions — a permanent assembly where the world's religions and spiritual communities will gather on a daily basis, in prayer, meditation, dialogue, and cooperative action, to make peace among religions so they might be a force for peace among nations, for addressing urgent human need, and for healing the earth.

World Conference on Religion and Peace
777 United Nations Plaza
New York, NY 10017
Tel: (212) 687-2163
Fax: (212) 983-0566
E-mail: info@wcrp.org

A global movement, with chapters in more than thirty countries; engages in peace initiatives and peace-related activities throughout the world. Works with U.N. agencies, and vigorously promotes multireligious cooperation to resolve conflicts, encourage sustainable development, and further human rights.

CHAPTER TWO: *The Caring Connection*

Big Brothers Big Sisters of America
National Office:
230 N. 13th St.
Philadelphia, PA 19107-1538
Tel (215) 567-7000
Fax: (215) 567-0394
E-mail: bbbsa@aol.com

Website: http://www.bbbsa.org
This is the nation's oldest youth mentoring organization. Matching an adult mentor with a child, they serve over 100,000 youth. With over 500 agencies across the country, their goal is to keep growing, so that more and more children will benefit from having a Big Brother or Big Sister.

Bread for the Journey
267 Miller Ave.
Mill Valley, CA 94941
Tel: (415) 383-4600
E-mail: wrmuller@aol.com and rheckler@sonic.net
Website: http://www.breadforthejourney.org
Nationally based organization that helps local people distribute funds at the grassroots community level to persons or organizations in need.

Children's Defense Fund
25 E. St., N.W.
Washington, D.C. 20001
Tel: (202) 628-8787
Fax: (202) 662-3510
E-mail: cdfinfo@childrensdefense.org
Website: http://www.childrensdefense.org
National children's advocacy organization headed by Marian Wright Edelman.

Children Now
1212 Broadway
Oakland, CA 94612
Tel: (510) 763-2444
Also have offices in Los Angeles, Sacramento, and New York City
E-mail: children@childrennow.org
Website: http://www.childrennow.org
Children Now is a nonpartisan, independent voice for America's children, working to translate the nation's commitment to children and families into action. They are particularly concerned about poor or at-risk children.

Feed the Children
P.O. Box 36
Oklahoma City, OK 73101
Tel: (405) 942-0228
E-mail: ftc@telepath.com
Website: http://www.feedthechildren.com
An international Christian organization that provides food, clothing, educational supplies, medical equipment, and necessities to people who lack these essentials due to famine, war, or other calamities.

Foundation for Community Encouragement
P.O. Box 17210
Seattle, WA 98107-0910
Tel: (206) 784-9000
Fax: (206) 784-9077
E-mail: inquire@fce-community.org
Website: http://www.fce-community.org
Through workshops and consultation, the Foundation for Community Encouragement serves as a catalyst for individuals, groups, and organizations in the United States and abroad to learn the principles of true community: learning how to communicate with authenticity, deal with difficult issues, welcome and affirm diversity, bridge differences with integrity, and relate with compassion and respect.

Free the Children International
16 Thornbank Rd.
Thornhill, Ontario
Canada L4J 2A2
Tel: (905) 881-0863
Fax: (905) 881-1849
They have offices in Australia, Europe, India, and the U.S.
E-mail: freechild@clo.com
Website: http://freethechildren.org
An international youth organization founded by Craig Kielburger, which has established programs and activities to reduce the poverty and exploitation of children throughout the world, including children caught in hazardous and exploitative child labor. They also provide leadership skills and citizenship opportunities to youth.

The Global Fund for Women
425 Sherman Ave., Suite 300
Palo Alto, CA 94306-1823
Tel: (650) 853-8305
Fax: (650) 328-0384
E-mail: gfw@globalfundforwomen.org
Website: http://www.globalfundforwomen.org
The Global Fund for Women is a grant-making foundation that provides flexible, timely financial assistance to women's groups around the world. Their grants enable women to participate fully in all aspects of their societies. Since its inception in 1987, the fund has given nearly $8.5 million to 995 grassroots women's groups in 123 countries and territories.

Grameen Foundation USA
236 Massachusetts Ave., N.E., Suite 300
Washington, D.C. 20002
Tel: (202) 543-2636
Fax: (202) 543-7512
E-mail: grameen_foundation@msn.com
Website: http://www.grameenfoundation.com
Established by Professor Muhammad Yunus, this foundation serves as an all-purpose resource center to educate policy makers and the public about the potential of microcredit to reduce poverty in the developing and industrialized world. It also provides technical support to microcredit programs modeled on the Grameen Bank.

Habitat for Humanity International
121 Habitat St.
Americus, GA 31709
Tel: (912) 924-6935
Fax: (912) 924-6541
E-mail: info@habitat.org
Website: http://www.habitat.org
An ecumenical Christian housing ministry, made famous through President Jimmy Carter's support, which seeks to eliminate homelessness. They consider a decent shelter "a matter of conscience and action," and therefore invite people from all walks of life to work together to build houses all around the world for families in need.

HOPE for Kids
5839 Green Calley Circle, Suite 203
Culver City, CA 90230
Tel: (310) 665-0888
Fax: (310) 665-0878
E-mail: hfkjoe@pacbell.net

HOPE for Kids is a program of HOPE Worldwide, a charity that serves the poor in over 154 cities in 58 nations. HOPE for Kids is HOPE Worldwide's largest volunteer organization in the United States, working to meet the health and development needs of children; over 35,000 volunteers participate nationwide.

Independent Sector
1828 L Street, N.W., Suite 1200
Washington, D.C. 20036
Tel: (202) 223-8100
Fax: (202) 457-0609
Website: http://www.indepsec.org

A national coalition of voluntary organizations, foundations, and corporate giving programs. Their mission is to encourage giving and volunteering in a way that serves individuals, communities, and causes.

Institute of HeartMath
P.O. Box 1463
14700 West Park Ave.
Boulder Creek, CA 95006
Tel: (408) 338-8700
fax. (408) 338-9861
E-mail: hrtmath@netcom.com
Website: http://www.heartmath.org

A corporation that specializes in scientific research and training programs. The Institute of HeartMath is a pioneer in biomedical research, showing the relationship between the heart, mental and emotional balance, cardiovascular function, and hormonal and immune system health. Their training programs, seminars, and retreats on individual and organizational effectiveness have been attended by Fortune 500 companies, educators, health care organizations, and branches of the Armed Forces.

MAD DADS

3030 Sprague St.
Omaha, NE 68111
Tel: (402) 451-3366
Fax: (402) 451-3477
E-mail: maddadsnational@nfinity.com
Website: http://www.maddadsnational.com

This organization works in more than fourteen states and fifty-three cities. Mobilizes local fathers to conduct street patrols to accomplish their acronyms: Men Against Destruction, Defending Against Drugs and Social Disorder. They also have a "Mum's Division" at the same address.

Maryland Student Service Alliance

Maryland State Department of Education
200 West Baltimore St.
Baltimore, MD 21201
Tel: (410) 767-0358
Fax: (410) 333-2183
Website: http://sailor.lib.md.us/mssa/

Maryland was first in the nation to make "service learning" a part of its minimum state requirements for high school graduation. Their program puts theory into practice, building academic, life, and job skills. Offers teacher training manuals, videos, guides.

Microcredit Summit

236 Massachusetts Ave., N.E., Suite 300
Washington, D.C. 20002
Tel: (202) 546-1900
E-mail: microcredit@igc.apc.org
Website: http://www.microcreditsummit.org

They have launched a campaign to reach 100 million of the world's poorest families, especially the women of those families, so they receive credit for self-employment and other financial and business services by the year 2005. Their goal is to help the poorest families move out of poverty.

Save the Children

54 Wilton Rd.
Westport, CT 06881

Tel: (203) 221-4000
Fax: (203) 226-6709
Website: savethechildren.org
Save the Children is a member of the International Save the Children Alliance, a partnership of groups working with children and families in more than 100 nations throughout the world. Their mission is to make lasting, positive change in the lives of disadvantaged children.

Stand for Children
1834 Connecticut Ave., N.W.
Washington, D.C. 20009
Tel: (800) 663-4032
Fax: (202) 234-0217
E-mail: tellstand@stand.org
Website: http://www.stand.org
Stand for Children is a national organization helping grassroots children's activists build Children's Action Teams that improve children's lives through successful policy change, awareness-raising, and service initiatives.

Touch the Future
4350 Lime Ave.
Long Beach, CA 90807-2815
Tel: (562) 426-2627
Fax: (562) 427-8189
E-mail:ttfuture@aol.com
This organization is creating new adult models for the next generation of children, based on the belief that adults place limitations on childhood — not children. Therefore, their goal is to help children discover and develop capacities far beyond the limitations most adults have accepted for themselves.

Violence Prevention Programs
Public Health Practice
Harvard School of Public Health
718 Huntington Ave.
Boston, MA 02115
Tel: (617) 432-2400

Fax: (617) 432-3050
E-mail: jkral@sph.harvard.edu
Website: http://www.hsph.harvard.edu/organizations/php/violence.html
The Violence Prevention Programs (VPP), housed within the Division of Public Health Practice at the Harvard School of Public Health, seek to provide innovative opportunities for developing programs, as well as evaluation strategies to ensure safer communities. VPP is an umbrella for several projects, including a national satellite training series with the National Coalition of Survivors for Violence Prevention. VPP is a far-reaching response to critical new developments and priorities in the field of public health.

CHAPTER THREE: *Healing Ourselves to Heal Society*

Academy for Guided Imagery
P.O. Box 2070
Mill Valley, CA 94942
Tel: (800) 726-2070
Fax: (415) 389-9342
E-mail: agi1996@aol.com
Website: http://www.healthy.net/agi
The mission of the Academy for Guided Imagery is to teach people to access and use the power of the mind/body connection for healing, growth, and creativity.

American Holistic Health Association
P.O. Box 17400
Anaheim, CA 92817-7400
Tel: (714) 779-6152
E-mail: ahha@healthy.net
Website: http://ahha.org
National clearinghouse for self-help resources promoting a holistic approach to wellness. AHHA offers, free of charge, a list of organizations that research information and treatment options on specific diseases or chronic conditions; the information covers both conventional and complementary treatments. They also offer a list of organizations that provide referrals to a wide variety of health care modalities, and list of free catalogs of health books and other self-help tools.

American Self-Help Clearinghouse
Northwest Covenant Medical Center
25 Pocono Rd.
Denville, NJ 07834
Tel: (973) 625-3037
Fax: (973) 625-8848
E-mail: ashc@cybernex.net
Website: http://www.cmhc.com/selfhelp
This clearinghouse assists individuals who wish to locate self-help groups
in their community. Also publishes *The Self-Help Sourcebook*, a national
directory of self-help groups.

Association for Humanistic Psychology
45 Franklin St., Suite 315
San Francisco, CA 94102
Tel: (415) 864-8850
Fax: (415) 864-8853
E-mail: ahpoffice@aol.com
Website: http://www.ahpweb.org
International community of people who are dedicated to the exploration
and healing of the human psyche, mind, and soul. Their mission: "To
realize a vision of the possible for humanity."

The Biofeedback and Psychophysiology Clinic
The Menninger Clinic
P.O. Box 829
Topeka, KS 66601-0829
Tel: (785) 350-5000
Website: http://www. menninger.edu
Teaches relaxation and self-awareness techniques to relieve stress-related
problems and other health concerns.

Center for Mind-Body Medicine
5225 Connecticut Ave., N.W., Suite 414
Washington, D.C. 20015
Tel: (202) 966-7338
Fax: (202) 966-2589
E-mail: cmbm@idsonline.com

Website: http://www.healthy.net/cmbm
Organization dedicated to creating a more compassionate, open-minded, and effective model of health care and health education. They conduct community education programs on mind-body techniques and training programs for health and mental health professionals. However, this center is not a treatment facility or referral service.

Center for Mindfulness/The Stress Reduction Clinic
University of Massachusetts Medical Center
55 Lake Ave. N.
Worcester, MA 01655
Tel: (508) 856-2656
Fax: (508) 856-1977
Offers courses in mindfulness-based stress reduction as a way of assisting people with chronic or acute medical conditions in tapping their own inner resources for health. Also provides professional training.

Confederation of Healing Organisations
The Red and White House
Suite J, Second Floor
113 High St.
Berkhamsted
Herts HP4 2DJ
England
Tel: (01442) 870660
Fax: (01442) 870667
The CHO is a registered charity and a founding member in the British Complementary Medicine Association, and member of the Healing Therapy Group. With its network of 7,000 healers, it is the largest complementary therapy organization in the UK. Healers must reach defined minimum standards for entry. Written inquiries should include a stamped addressed envelope to receive a reply.

Commonweal
P.O. Box 316
Bolinas, CA 94924
Tel: (415) 868-0970

Website: http://www.commonwealhealth.org
The Commonweal Cancer Help Program offers psychological support programs for cancer patients and conducts training programs in holistic therapies for health professionals who treat life-threatening illnesses.

Doctors Without Borders

6 E. 39th St., 8th floor
New York, NY 10016
Tel: (212) 679-6800
Fax: (212) 679-7016
E-mail: dwb@new york.msf.org
Website: http://www.dwb.org

Doctors Without Borders (known internationally as Médecins Sans Frontières and MSF) delivers emergency medical relief to populations whose health is threatened by war, civil strife, epidemics, or natural disasters. Its volunteers train and work closely with local staff. When medical assistance is not enough to save lives, Doctors Without Borders will speak out against human rights abuses and violations of international humanitarian law that its teams witness while providing medical relief. It is a network of nineteen national sections worldwide.

Gladys Taylor McGarey Medical Foundation

7350 E. Stetson Drive, Suite 120
Scottsdale, AZ 85251
Tel: (602) 946-4544
Fax: (602) 946-6902
E-mail: gtmmfihc@primenet.com
Website: http://www.primenet.com/~gtmmfihc

The mission of this foundation is to advance human understanding of the body-mind-spirit relationship and encourage wellness and wholeness through the combination of the best of conventional and holistic medical practices.

Health Frontiers Professional Network

6876 Pinehaven Rd.
Oakland, CA 94611
Tel: (510) 655-9951
Fax: (510) 654-6699

A forum for health care professionals and friends interested in clarifying and operating cost-effective models for health care based on patient centered, caring-based processes.

The Health Resource Inc.
564 Locust St.
Conway, AR 72032
Tel: (501) 329-5272
Fax: (501) 329-9489
E-mail: moreinfo@thehealthresource.com
International medical information service that provides individualized reports on specific medical conditions.

HealthWorld Online
Tel: (562) 862-6116
Website: http://www.healthy.net
This is the Internet's leading resource on health. It is a consumer friendly site that lists healing organizations, professional referrals, and holistic and complementary medicine information.

Institute of Transpersonal Psychology
744 San Antonio Rd.
Palo Alto, CA 94303
Tel: (650) 493-4430
Fax: (650) 493-6835
E-mail: itpinfo@best.com
Website: http://www.tmn.com/itp/
Professional graduate school that combines academic and experiential training in the psychology of wholeness, including personal and spiritual development.

International Healthy Cities Foundation —
See Holistic Organizations.

The Mind-Body Medical Institute
Beth Israel Deaconess Medical Center — West Campus
110 Francis St., Suite 1A

Boston, MA 02215
Tel: (617) 632-9530
Fax: (617) 632-7383
E-mail: mindbodymedicalclinic@bidmc.harvard.edu
Website: http://www.med.harvard.edu/programs/mind/body
Scientific and educational organization affiliated with Beth Israel
Deaconess Hospital and Harvard Medical School that conducts research
and disseminates findings regarding mind-body and complementary
healing practices.

Nurse Healers — Professional Associates Inc.
1211 Locust St.
Philadelphia, PA 19107
Tel: (215) 545- 8079
Fax: (215) 545-8107
E-mail: nhpa@nursecominc.com
Website: http://www.therapeutic-touch.org
Membership organization that offers Therapeutic Touch workshops, and
information on Therapeutic Touch practitioners. Their mission: "To fur-
ther the use of healing modalities."

Physicians for Social Responsibility
1101 Fourteenth St., N.W., Suite 700
Washington, D.C. 20005
Tel: (202) 898-0150
Fax: (202) 898-0172
E-mail: psrnatl@psr.org
Website: http://www.psr.org
National organization committed to the ultimate abolition of all nuclear
weapons and to eliminating threats to public health and the environment.

Planetree Health Resource Center
Institute for Health and Healing
2040 Webster St.
San Francisco, CA 94115
Tel: (415) 923-3680
Fax: (415) 673-2629
E-mail: ihhlib@sirius.com

Consumer health library free to public; offers conventional and alternative health care information, walk-in or by mail.

Preventive Medicine Research Institute
900 Bridgeway, Suite 1
Sausalito, CA 94965
Tel: (415) 332-2525
Fax: (415) 332-5730
Website: http://www.ornish.com
Public institute, founded by Dean Ornish, that is dedicated to research, service, and education.

Psychologists for Social Responsibility
2607 Connecticut Ave., N.W.
Washington, D.C. 20008
Tel: (202) 745-7084
Fax: (202) 745-0051
E-mail: psysrusa@interserv.com
Website: http://www.rmc.edu/psysr
International membership organization for psychologists and nonpsychologists. This worldwide network's mission is to "reorient thinking, behavior, and values to foster peaceful communities."

Simonton Cancer Center
P.O. Box 890
Pacific Palisades, CA 90272
Tel: (800) 459-3424 or (310) 459-4994
Tel. for tapes and literature: (800) 388-2360
Fax: (310) 457-0421
E-mail: simonton@lainet.com
Website: http://www.2.lainet.com/"simonton/checkhit.htm
Pioneered by Dr. Carl Simonton, the center treats cancer patients and trains professionals in the use of imagery with cancer patients.

Shakti Foundation
P.O. Box 151721
San Rafael, CA 94915
Tel: (415) 454-7223

The primary focus of the Shakti Foundation is to serve low-income women living with breast cancer or any other life-threatening illness. They offer emotional, physical, psychological and spiritual help for women by funding access to complementary healing options, fostering a community of compassion and action, and providing direct service and education.

The Wellness Community
2716 Ocean Park Blvd., Suite 1040
Santa Monica, CA 90405
Tel: (310) 314-2555
Fax: (310) 314-7586
E-mail: wellness@beachnet.com

Provides free psychological and emotional support to cancer patients and their family members. Seventeen locations across the country.

World Health Foundation
Medigrace
140 High St. #6
Ashland, OR 97520
Tel: (541) 488-2563
E-mail: medgrace@mind.net
Website: http://www.mind.net/medigrace

The foundation's goal is to advance the use of meditation in medicine. It has established programs in the medical applications of meditation, with special programs for cancer and childbirth.

The World Research Foundation
The World Research Building
41 Bell Rock Plaza
Sedona, AZ 86351
Tel: (520) 284-3300
Fax: (520) 284-3530
E-mail: wrf@wrf.org
Website: http://wrf.org

They gather information on potential forms of therapy, both traditional and nontraditional, for people to explore their options. Publishes quarterly newsletter. Offices in Europe and the People's Republic of China.

CHAPTER FOUR: *Working to Benefit Society*

Business for Social Responsibility
609 Mission St., 2nd floor
San Francisco, CA 94105
Tel: (415) 537-0888
Fax: (415) 537-0889
Website: http://www.bsr.org
Business for Social Responsibility's (BSR) mission is to help member companies implement policies and practices that contribute to their long-term success, honor high ethical standards, and meet the company's responsibilities to its various stakeholders. The BSR Education Fund is an affiliated nonprofit organization that promotes more responsible practices in the broader business community, and increases support for responsible business practices in our society.

The Center for a New American Dream
6930 Carroll Ave., Suite 900
Takoma Park, MD 20912
Tel: (301) 891-3683
Fax: (301) 891-3684
E-mail: newdream@newdream.org
Website: http://www.newdream.org
The Center for a New American Dream works to promote more fulfilling and sustainable lifestyles while shifting our patterns of material resource consumption. The national educational organization encourages people to reconnect with families and communities and ask, "How much is enough?"

Center for Ethics and Economic Policy
2512 9th St., Suite 3
Berkeley, CA 94710-2542
Tel: (510) 549-9931
Fax: (510) 549-9995
E-Mail: ethicsecon@aol.com
The center offers values-based economic training and leadership development to organizations wishing to further their own goals of social change.

Center for Popular Economics
P.O. Box 785
Amherst, MA 01004
Tel: (413) 545-0743
Fax: (413) 545-2921
E-mail: cpe@acad.umass.edu
Through their publications and workshops they teach economic literacy to activists and educators, with the goal of preventing social issues from being distorted by economic jargon.

Conscious Business Alliance
4243 Grimes Ave., S.
Edina, Minnesota 55146
Tel: (612) 925-5995
Fax: (612) 920-7168
E-mail: hilnc@aol.com
Website: http://www.real.org/hp/cba
An international membership alliance of businesses, organizations, and individuals committed to bringing higher values and meaning to the workplace.

Council on Economic Priorities
30 Irving Place
New York, NY 10003-2386
Tel: (212) 420-1133
Fax: (212) 420-0988
Also offers SCREEN research service for investors
E-mail: cep@echonyc.com
Website: http://accesspt.com/cep/
Founded in 1969, the Council on Economic Priorities (CEP) is a non-profit public service research organization that provides accurate and impartial analysis of the social and environmental records of corporations. This research is designed to enhance the incentives for corporate social and environmental performance. CEP information empowers consumers, investors, managers, employees, and activists to cast their economic vote as conscientiously as their political vote.

E.F. Schumacher Society
140 Jug End Rd.
Great Barrington, MA 01230
Tel: (413) 528-1737
Fax: (413) 528-4472
E-mail: efssociety@aol.com
Website: http://www.schumachersociety.org

Their resource library and programs provide tools to strengthen local economies and build sustainable communities; they specialize in community land trusts and local currencies.

Families and Work Institute
330 Seventh Ave.
New York, NY 10001
Tel: (212) 465-2044
Fax: (212) 465-8637
Website: http://www.familiesandwork.org

This institute addresses the changing nature of work and family life. They are committed to finding research-based strategies that foster mutually supportive connections among workplaces, families, and communities. The institute identifies emerging work-life issues, benchmarks solutions to work-life problems, and evaluates the impact of solutions on employees, their families, and communities.

Graduation Pledge Alliance
MC Box 135
Manchester College
North Manchester, IN 46962
E-mail: njwollman@manchester.edu

Students pledge to "investigate and take into account the social and environmental consequences of any job opportunity." Contact this address for an explanatory brochure, and information about how to start a Graduation Pledge effort at your college or university.

The Harwood Group
4915 St. Elmo Ave., Suite 402
Bethesda, MD 20814

Tel: (301) 656-3669
Fax: (301) 656-0533
E-mail: harwoodgrp@aol.com
Website: http://www.thg@hardwoodgroup.com/

The Harwood Group is a lab for public innovation and is part of the Harwood family of organizations. It works with citizens, communities, civic organizations, and institutions to gain an understanding of society's challenges, and how to create effective action around those challenges. In 1998, the Harwood Institute was chartered as a nonprofit network for public ideas, with the purpose of bringing people together to initiate progress in the public realm.

Institute for Women's Policy Research

1400 20th St., N.W., Suite 104
Washington, D.C. 20036
Tel: (202) 785-5100
Website: http://www.iwpr.org

Independent scientific research organization established to inform and stimulate debate on issues critical to women. Their research addresses issues of race and ethnicity, and specifically promotes policies that help low-income women achieve self-sufficiency and autonomy.

Interfaith Center on Corporate Responsibility

475 Riverside Dr., Room 550
New York, NY 10115
Tel: (212) 870-2295
E-mail: info@iccr.org

Membership organization that advocates socially responsible investing and corporate social and environmental responsibility.

International Alliance of Holistic Lawyers

P.O. Box 753
Middlebury, VT 05753
Tel: (802) 388-7478
Fax: (802) 388-4079
E-mail: lawyer@holistic.com

Website: http://www.holistic.com
The International Alliance of Holistic Lawyers is an organization of lawyers, law students, mediators, and others dedicated to the evolution of how the justice and legal professions are defined, practiced, and perceived by both its practitioners and clientele. The term "holistic" means they incorporate the whole of an event — the patterns and history that brought the parties into conflict, the motivations that compelled the action, and the impacts and effects that naturally and lawfully follow.

The New Road Map Foundation
P.O. Box 15981
Seattle, WA 98115
Tel: (206) 527-0437
Fax: (206) 528-1120
Website: http://www.slnet.com/cip/nrm
An all-volunteer educational and charitable organization concerned with the role of personal responsibility and personal initiative in effecting positive global changes. Most of their work is focused on finance and sustainable lifestyles, since they believe that economic issues and our relationship with money are central to both personal and planetary well-being. Their educational programs support the evolution of culture as well as the empowerment of individuals.

Redefining Progress
One Kearny St., 4th floor
San Francisco, CA 94108
Tel: (415) 781-1191
Fax (415) 781-1198
E-mail: info@rprogress.org
Website: http://www.rprogress.org
Redefining Progress (RP) is a public policy organization that seeks to ensure a more sustainable and socially equitable world. Working both within and beyond the traditional economic framework, RP generates and refines innovative policies and ideas that balance economic well-being, the environment, and social equity so that those living today and in the future can have a better quality of life.

The Shorter Work-Time Group
69 Dover St.
Somerville, MA 02144
Tel: (617) 628-5558

Founded in 1989, the Shorter Work-Time Group challenges our nation's workaholic culture and workplace policies, and promotes the right of all people, of all occupations and income levels, to earn a decent living while spending less time doing paid work. They promote this goal through their publications, conferences, and other educational programs.

Social Venture Network
P.O. Box 29221
San Francisco, CA 94129-0221
Tel: (415) 561-6501
Fax: (415) 561-6435
E-mail: svn@wenet.net
Website: http://www.svn.org

Social Venture Network is a membership organization of successful business and social entrepreneurs dedicated to promoting a more just, humane, and sustainable society by changing the way the world does business and by supporting progressive solutions to social problems.

Society for the Advancement of Socio-Economics
P.O. Box 39008
Baltimore, MD 21212
Tel: (410) 377-7965
E-mail: saseorg@aol.com

An international network of academicians, business people, policy makers and anyone interested in the fusion of economics and all disciplines. They approach economics not as self-contained system but as a whole system influenced by values and numerous noneconomic factors.

The Trends Research Institute
Salisbury Turnpike
Rhinebeck, NY 12572
Tel: (914) 876-6700
Fax: (914) 758-5252
Website: http://www.trendsresearch.com

The Trends Research Institute, founded in 1980, combines their resources with their own trademarked methodology to help companies profit from trends.

For information about **Voluntary Simplicity** programs contact:
Education Program
c/o Phinney Neighborhood Association
6532 Phinney Ave., N.
Seattle, WA 98103
Tel: (206) 783-2244
Fax: (206) 783-2246
E-mail: pnacenter@aol.com
Website: http://www.poppyware.com/pna/
This association has organized Voluntary Simplicity classes in the Seattle area. Check website or mail a self-addressed stamped envelope for information. Or contact these three offices for more information about Voluntary Simplicity:

Learning for Life Project
711 North 60th
Seattle, WA 98103
Tel: (206) 782-5105
Fax: (206) 781-1041
E-Mail: andrews@igc.apc.org

Simple Living Journal
2319 N. 45th, Box 149
Seattle, WA 98103
Tel: (206) 464-4800

Study Circles Resource Center
P.O. Box 203
697 Pomfret St.
Pomfret, CT 06258
Tel: (860) 928-2616
Fax: (860) 928-3713
E-mail: scrc@neca.com

The Whole Life Economics Network
P.O. Box 44-1615
Somerville, MA 02144
Tel: (617) 628-5558

Network for exploring and participating in a sustainable community economic paradigms.

Workways
57 Henry St.
Cambridge, MA 02139
Tel: (617) 661-3518
E-mail: hsussman@earthlink.net
Website: http://home.earthlink.net/~hsussman
Harris Sussman and Workways Consulting specialize in helping develop organizations as social systems for quantum learning, cultural diversity, and creativity. Workways provides executive coaching and interventions to groups in all sectors and disciplines.

World Business Academy
P.O. Box 191210
San Francisco, CA 94119-1210
Tel: (415) 227-0106
Fax: (415) 227-0561
E-mail: wba@well.com
Website: http://www.worldbusiness.org
The academy is a global network of business executives and entrepreneurs who are motivated to help bring about the smooth transformation of business — working toward a humane, ecologically sound, and spiritually satisfying future.

CHAPTER FIVE: *Whole Ways to Learn*

Accelerated Schools Project
Stanford University
CERAS Building
Stanford, CA 94305-3084
Tel: (415) 725-1676 (information packet only)
Website: http://www-leland.stanford.edu/group/ASP
The Accelerated Schools Project was launched at Stanford University in 1986 as a comprehensive approach to school change, designed to improve schooling for children in "at-risk" situations. Instead of placing

students in remedial classes, the accelerated school communities — staff, parents, students, and local community members — accelerate student learning by providing all students with challenging activities that traditionally have been reserved for students identified as gifted.

Campus Compact
c/o Brown University
P.O. Box 1975
Providence, RI 02912
Tel: (401) 863-1119
Fax: (401) 863-3799
E-mail: campus@compact.org
Website: http://www.compact.org
A national membership organization of college and university presidents committed to helping students develop the values and skills of citizenship through participation in public and community service. It is the first national higher education organization whose primary purpose is to support campus-based public and community service.

Center for the Advancement of Ethics and Character
Character Education Network
School of Education
Boston University
605 Commonwealth Ave.
Boston, MA 02215
Tel: (617) 353-3262
Fax: (617) 353-3924
Website: http://education.bu.edu/charactered/
A center that focuses on the education of teachers, providing resources and a philosophical framework to help educators teach high moral ideals. They are the authors of a "Character Education Manifesto," a one-page statement defining the core principles of character education. This statement has been signed by forty renowned educational leaders.

Center for the 4th and 5th Rs
Education Department
SUNY Cortland
P.O. Box 2000

Cortland, NY 13045
Tel: (607) 753-2455
Fax: (607) 753-5980
E-mail: c4n5rs@cortland.edu
Website: http://www.cortland.edu/www/c4n5rs

Founded and directed by Thomas Lickona, this center acts as a regional, state, and national resource for character education; helps schools, teachers, and parents develop good character in youth. Holds an annual K-12 Summer Institute in Character Education, and conferences on High School Character Education. They also publish a newsletter and disseminate complimentary information packets on character education and character-based sex education.

Center for Learning

21590 Center Ridge Rd.
Rocky River, OH 44116
Tel: (440) 331-1404
Fax: (440) 331-5414
E-mail: cfl@stratos.net
Website: http://www.centerforlearning.org

Committed to the advancement of academic learning and the integration of ethical values in education, they produce and distribute educational materials to an international market, and sponsor in-service programs.

Child Development Project

Developmental Studies Center
2000 Embarcadero, Suite 305
Oakland, CA 94606
Tel: (510) 533-0213
Fax: (510) 464-3670
Website: http://www.devstu.org

Formed in 1980, the Child Development Project conducts research and develops school-based programs that foster children's intellectual, ethical, and social development. Their mission is to deepen children's commitment to being kind, helpful, responsible, and respectful of others — qualities essential to leading humane and productive lives in a democratic society.

Character Education Partnership
918 16th St., N.W., Suite 501
Washington, D.C. 20006
Tel: (202) 296-7743
Fax: (202) 296-7779
Website: http://www.character.org
A nonpartisan coalition of organizations and individuals active in developing moral character, providing schools with the tools and resources they need to enhance character education programs.

The Council for Global Education
P.O. Box 57218
Washington, D.C. 20036-9998
Tel: (202) 496-9780
Fax: (202) 496-9781
E-mail: info@globaleducation.org
Website: http://www.globaleducation.org
An international educational institution dedicated to promoting the development of the whole child. Its primary purpose is to provide children with the moral foundation, intellectual skills, and wisdom necessary to deal with today's complex problems and to lead a fulfilling life.

Educators for Social Responsibility
23 Garden St.
Cambridge, MA 02138
Tel: (617) 492-1764
Fax: (617) 864-5164
E-mail: educators@esrnational.org
Website: http://www.benjerry.com/esr
Professional association of educators formed to help young people develop the convictions and skills to shape a safe, sustainable, and just world. They offer curriculum materials, workshops, and train teachers in conflict resolution techniques.

Ethics Resource Center
1747 Pennsylvania Ave., N.W., Suite 400
Washington, D.C. 20006

Tel: (202) 737-2258
Fax: (202) 737-2227
E-mail: ethics@ethics.org
Website: http://www.ethics.org

Nonpartisan, nonsectarian organization with the mission to serve as a catalyst to improve the ethical practices of individuals and organizations from the classroom to the boardroom. They offer organizational/business ethics consulting, facilitate character education programs, and act as an ethics information clearinghouse.

The Giraffe Program: Character Education and
Service-Learning Curriculum Guide
P.O. Box 759
Langley, WA 98260
Tel: (360) 221-7989
Fax: (360) 221-7817
E-mail: office@giraffe.org
Website: http://www.giraffe.org/giraffe/

The program is a K-12 curriculum fostering courage, caring, and personal responsibility in students. It is implemented by individual teachers and through alliances with such organizations as Cities In Schools and the U.S. Navy.

Heartwood Institute
425 N. Craig St., Suite 302
Pittsburgh, PA 15213
Tel: (800) 432-7810 or (412) 688-8570
Fax: (412) 688-8552
E-mail: hrtwood@aol.com
Website: http://www.envirolink.org/orgs/heartwood

Organization that offers a multicultural, literature-based ethics curriculum designed to present universal values to children from early childhood to sixth grade. Information is available to schools, day-care centers, organizations, and the general public.

The Institute for Global Ethics

P.O. Box 563
Camden, ME 04843
Tel: (207) 236-6658
Fax: (207) 236-4014
E-mail: ethics@globalethics.org
Website: http://www.globalethics.org

London office:
16 Northwick Close
London NW8 8JG
England
northwick@easynet.co.uk

An international, membership-based, independent, nonsectarian, nonpolitical, think tank dedicated to promoting the discussion of ethics in a global context. The Institute works with schools, state departments of education, and educational organizations, providing ethics training, seminars, and consulting.

Josephson Institute of Ethics

Character Counts! Coalition
4640 Admiralty Way, Suite 1001
Marina del Rey, CA 90292-6610
Tel: (310) 306-1868
Fax: (310) 827-1864
E-mail: jistaff@jiethics.org
Website: http://www.josephsoninstitute.org

Nationwide nonpartisan, nonsectarian alliance of over 250 schools and nonprofit organizations devoted to developing the character of young people.

Learning Styles Network

Center for the Study of Learning and Teaching Styles
St. John's University
8000 Utopia Parkway
Jamaica, NY 11439
Tel: (718) 990-6335
Fax: (718) 990-6096

The first Learning Styles Network was formed in 1979 through an agreement between St. John's University and the national association of secondary school principals. Today, network centers exist throughout the United States (Alabama, North Carolina, Florida, Michigan, New York, Texas, Virginia, Ohio, Oklahoma) as well as in Finland, the Philippines, and New Zealand.

New Horizons for Learning
P.O. Box 15329
Seattle, WA 98115-0329
Tel: (206) 547-7936
Fax: (206) 547-0328
E-mail: building@newhorizons.org
Website: http://www.newhorizons.org

International education network. Their website is a rich resource, designed as an elaborate "building" with floors devoted to a monthly electronic newsletter, plus information on restructuring K-12, early childhood education, parent education, effective teaching practices, learning in the workplace, international news, and ideas for the future.

Personal Responsibility Education Process (PREP)
Cooperating School Districts of Greater St. Louis
8225 Florissant Rd.
St. Louis, MO 63121
Tel: (314) 516-4528
Fax: (314) 516-4599
E-mail: lindam@info.csd.org
Website: http://info.csd.org

The Cooperating School Districts (CSD) is an educational consortium that provides staff development, cooperative purchasing, educational technology, and legislative and financial services to public school districts in the greater St. Louis metropolitan area. The Personal Responsibility Education Process (PREP), a project of the CSD, is one of the nation's largest school-business-community partnerships in character education. Started in 1988, PREP's mission is to integrate character education into curricula, discipline policies, after-school activities, and school reform initiatives. PREP currently involves over 400 schools.

The Robert Muller School
International Coordinating Center
6005 Royal Oak Dr.
Arlington, TX 76016-1035
Tel: (817) 654-1018
Fax: (817) 654-1028

E-mail: rmswcc@airmail.net
Website: http://www.unol.org

Dr. Robert Muller, former assistant secretary-general of the United Nations, has initiated "The World Core Curriculum" to give students from birth through high school an inclusive and unprejudiced view of the world, and to expand all academics to fit into that view. Students are taught how to respect and appreciate all humankind, our differences as well as similarities, and to assess the contribution they can make to improve life.

Roots & Shoots

International education program, affiliated with the Jane Goodall Institute, where children work on solutions to local problems, and through the program's activities, learn to care about and respect all living things. For address, see Chapter Six Resource Guide.

CHAPTER SIX: *The Environmental Connection*

Center for Ecoliteracy

2522 San Pablo Ave.
Berkeley, CA 94702
Tel: 510-845-4595
Fax: 510-845-1439

The Center for Ecoliteracy is dedicated to fostering ecological literacy — the understanding and practice of the principles of ecology, the "language of nature" — through a grant-giving program and educational activities.

Center for Neighborhood Technology

2125 W. North Ave.
Chicago, IL 60647
Tel: (773) 278-4800
E-mail: info@cnt.org
Website: http://www.cnt.org

An organization founded in 1978 by Scott Bernstein to promote sustainable development, community building, and environmental solutions in cities at the local, neighborhood level. CNT publishes *The Neighborhood Works*, an award-winning magazine with the same mission.

Children's Health Environmental Coalition (CHEC)
P.O. Box 846
Malibu, CA 90265
Tel: (310) 573-9608
Fax: (310) 573-9688
E-mail: chec@checnet.org
Website: http://www.checnet.org
CHEC is a network of concerned parents and grassroots groups across the nation. Their goal is to eliminate children's exposure to man-made toxic substances, thus reducing children's risk of developing cancer, developmental disorders, and neurological defects.

EnviroLink Network
Website: http://www.envirolink.org
The largest online environmental information resource on the planet. This grassroots online community unites hundreds of organizations and volunteers around the world.

The Garden Project
Pier 28
The Embarcadero
San Francisco, CA 94105
Tel: (415) 243-8558
Cathrine Sneed is the founder of the Garden Project at the San Francisco County Jail. Using the Garden Project as a model, the U.S. Department of Agriculture has produced a manual for people who wish to pursue their own projects to help prisoners or disfranchised individuals.

GENI — Global Energy Network International
P.O. Box 81565
San Diego, CA 92138
Tel: (619) 595-0139
Fax: (619) 595-0403
E-mail: geni@cerf.net
Website: http://www.geni.org/
Conducts research and education into the benefits of interconnecting electrical networks between regions, with a focus on tapping renewable energy resources. This strategy is based on the premier solution for peace

and sustainable development from the World Game, designed by Dr. R. Buckminster Fuller.

The Global Citizen
Donella Meadows
Dartmouth College
Environmental Studies
305A Steele H B 6182
Hanover, NH 03755

Professor Donella Meadows writes syndicated articles presenting "a global view, a connected view, a long-term view, an environmental and compassionate view."

The Goldman Environmental Foundation
One Lombard St., Suite 303
San Francisco, CA 94111
Tel: (415) 788-9090
Fax: (415) 788-7890
E-mail: gef@igc.apc.org
Website: http://www.goldmanprize.org/goldman/

Presents annual environmental awards to reward individuals for outstanding grassroots environmental actions around the world, with the hope that these awards will draw public attention to critical environmental problems, and inspire others to act.

The Jane Goodall Institute for Wildlife Research, Education, and Conservation
(also to contact **Roots & Shoots**)
P.O. Box 14890
Silver Spring
Maryland 20911
Tel: (800) 592-JANE
Website: http://www.wcsu.ctstateu.edu/cyberchimp/

The Jane Goodall Institute (JGI), founded in 1977, is committed to wildlife research and conservation, particularly of chimpanzees. They investigate and publicize the endangered status of chimpanzees in the wild and the sometimes deplorable conditions to which they are subjected in captivity. In addition, JGI has established the Roots & Shoots program for young people, from the kindergarten to university level. This program teaches young people how to work on solutions to local problems, and through these activities learn to care about all living things.

Roots & Shoots Offices Worldwide:
JGI-UK: 15 Clarendon Park, Lymington, Hants SO41 8AX.
JGI-Canada: 5165 Sherbrooke St. West, Suite 408, Montreal, Quebec, H4A IT6
JGI-Tanzania: P.O. Box 727, Dar es Salaam, Tanzania, East Africa
JGI-Europe: Contact U.K. or U.S. office

Greenpeace International
Keizersgracht 176
1016 DW Amsterdam
Netherlands
Tel: 31 20 523 6222
Fax: 31 20 523 6200

Greenpeace USA
1436 U St., N.W.
Washington, D.C. 20009
Tel: (202) 462-1177
Fax: (202) 462-4507
Website: http:www. greenpeaceusa.org
International website: http://www.greenpeace.org
An international, independent campaigning organization that uses nonviolent, creative confrontation to expose global environmental problems, and to drive solutions essential to a sustainable future. They seek to protect biodiversity in all its forms; prevent pollution and the abuse of oceans, land, air, and fresh water; and promote peace, global disarmament, and nonviolence.

Institute for Deep Ecology
P.O. Box 1050
Occidental, CA 95465

Tel: (707) 874-2347
Fax: (707) 874-2367
E-mail: ide@igc.org

The institute offers ecology trainings to explore new ways of bringing ecological perspectives into personal, professional, and community life. Their trainings are grounded in a belief in the essential value and interdependence of all forms of being.

The Land Institute

2440 East Water Well Rd.
Salina, KS 67401
Tel: (785) 823-5376
Fax: (785) 823-8728
E-mail: theland@midkan.com
Website: http://www.midkan.com/the land/

Founded by Wes and Dana Jackson, this organization is dedicated to the search for principles of a natural-system agriculture for human and animal food. The Land Institute also explores principles for rural agricultural human communities by respecting and adapting to the limits of their ecosystems.

National Religious Partnership for the Environment

1047 Amsterdam Ave.
New York, NY 10025
Tel: (212) 316-7441
Fax: (212) 316-7547
E-mail: nrpe@aol.com
Website: http://www.nrpe.org

The National Religious Partnership for the Environment is a federation of major American faith communities: the U.S. Catholic Conference, the Coalition on the Environment and Jewish Life, the National Council of Churches of Christ, and the Evangelical Environmental Network. With a commitment "to be ourselves, together," each of the faith groups is implementing distinctive programs on behalf of a common mission: to integrate their commitment to global sustainability and environmental justice into all aspects of religious life.

The Natural Step
Thoreau Center for Sustainability
P.O. Box 29372
San Francisco, CA 94129-0372
Tel: (415) 561-3344
Fax: (415) 561-3345
E-mail: tns@naturalstep.org
Website: http://www.emis.com/tns

An educational organization, the Natural Step is both a conceptual framework and a guide to action that teaches science-based system conditions for sustainability that can be used as a compass to lead businesses, governments, communities, and academic institutions toward a sustainable future.

Natural Resources Defense Council
40 W. 20th St.
New York, NY 10011
Tel: (212) 727-2700
E-mail: nrdcinfo@nrdc.org
Website: http://www.nrdc.org

A national organization formed to protect the world's natural resources and ensure a safe and healthy environment for all people. With more than 350,000 members and a staff of lawyers, scientists, and environmental specialists, they combine the power of law, the power of science, and the power of people in defense of the environment.

Population Action International
1120 19th St., N.W., Suite 550
Washington, D.C. 20036-3606
Tel: (202) 659-1833
Fax: (202) 293-1795
E-mail: pai@popact.org
Website: http://www.populationaction.org

Population Action International is dedicated to advancing policies and programs that slow population growth in order to enhance the quality of life for all people.

Sierra Club
National Headquarters:
85 2nd St., 2nd floor
San Francisco, CA 94105
Tel: (415) 977-5500
E-mail: information@sierraclub.org
Website: http://www.sierraclub.org

Sierra Club Canada
1 Nicholas St., Suite 620
Ottowa, Ontario
Canada, KIN 7B7
Tel: (613) 241-4611
This well-known environmental group, founded in 1892, is a member-supported public interest organization that promotes conservation of the natural environment by influencing public policy decisions. They have 550,000 members, 65 chapters, and 396 groups.

Urban Ecology
405 14th St., Suite 900
Oakland, CA 94612-2706
Tel: (510) 251-6330
Fax: (510) 251-2117
E-mail: urbanecology@igc.apc.org
Website: http://www.best.com/~schmitty/ueindex.shtml
or
Urban Ecology Australia Inc.
84 Halifax St.
Adeliaide, Tandanya Bioregion
SA 5000 Australia
Tel: 61-8-8232-4866
Website: http://www.eastend.com.au/~ecology/index.shtml
This membership organization founded in 1975 promotes environmentally sustainable and socially just communities by working on four levels: educating individuals though publications, forums, and tours; local land-use policy reform through their Realize the Vision Program; a community design consulting program; and planning of sustainable

regions, with a focus on the San Francisco Bay Area. Their quarterly journal, *The Urban Ecologist*, has an international readership.

Urban Habitat Program
P.O. Box 29908
Presidio Station
San Francisco, CA 94129
Tel: (415) 561-3333
Fax: (415) 561-3334
E-mail: uhp@igc.apc.org
Website: http://www.igc.org/uhp

The Urban Habitat Program's mission is to promote the development of multicultural, multiracial environmental leadership for building sustainable, socially just communities in the San Francisco Bay Area. They publish *Race, Poverty, and the Environment* magazine.

World Wildlife Fund
1250 24th St., N.W.
Washington, D.C. 20037
Tel: (202) 293-4800
Fax: (202) 293-9211
Website: http://www.wwf.org

Membership organization involved in international efforts to protect the diversity of life on earth.

Worldwatch Institute
1776 Massachusetts Ave., N.W.
Washington, D.C. 20036
Tel: (202) 452-1999
Fax: (202) 296-7365
E-mail: worldwatch@worldwatch.org
Website: http://www.worldwatch.org

Founded in 1974, the Worldwatch Institute is an independent public policy research institute. They conduct interdisciplinary, nonpartisan research on emerging global environmental issues, the results of which are disseminated throughout the world. Their mission is to raise public awareness of global environmental threats and elicit effective policy responses. The goal is to foster an environmentally sustainable society, one in which human needs are met in ways that do not threaten the health of the natural environment or the prospects of future generations. Publications by the Worldwatch Institute: the bimonthly *World Watch* magazine, the annual *State of the World* book, the annual *Vital Signs* book, Worldwatch papers, and monographs.

Zero Population Growth
1400 Sixteenth St., N.W.
Washington, D.C. 20036
Tel: (202) 332-2200, (800) 767-1956
Fax: (202) 332-2302
E-mail: zpg@igc.org
Website: http:// www.zpg.org

An environmental organization that educates people about the impact of rapid population growth, ZPG's 60,000 members work on issues as diverse as tackling urban sprawl and curbing teen pregnancy. Its nation-wide education and advocacy effort includes training 4,500 teachers every year.

CHAPTER SEVEN: *Living as a Work of Art*

Americans for the Arts
1000 Vermont Ave., N.W., 12th floor
Washington, D.C. 20005
Tel: (202) 371-2830
Fax: (202) 371-0424
Website: http://www.artsusa.org

National membership organization formed to support the arts and culture through private and public resource development, public policy development, information services, and public education.

The American News Service
289 Fox Farm Rd.
P.O. Box 8187
Brattleboro, VT 05304
Tel: (800) 654-NEWS

Fax: (802) 254-1227
Website: http://www.americannews.com
A news service that finds success stories and offers them to the mainstream media to counteract negative news. Founded by Frances Moore Lappé and Paul Martin Du Bois.

Artship Foundation
1749 Middle Harbor Rd., Building D-834
Oakland, CA 94607
Tel: (510) 272-4879
Fax: (510) 238-5104
E-mail: artship@aol.com
A community foundation committed to developing a creative arts and cultural education center at the Oakland waterfront, which will be one of the most visible and highly utilized cultural and educational centers for residents and visitors. The Artship Foundation was also chosen as the site for the future United States campus of the International Peace University (IPU), currently based in Berlin. IPU is sponsored by a board of directors and advisors that includes thirteen Nobel Peace Prize laureates.

Association for Music and Imagery
1525 Laurent St.
Santa Cruz, CA 95060
Tel: (408) 426-8937
Fax: (408) 423-7230
The Association for Music and Imagery was created to maintain and uphold the integrity of the Bonny Method of Guided Imagery and Music, and to nurture and support its members. The organization certifies those qualified to teach the Bonny Method and establishes the content of their training programs. They publish a professional journal each year and a semi-annual newsletter.

The Bonny Foundation
2020 Simmons St.
Salina, KS 67401
Tel: (785) 827-1497
Fax: (785) 827-5706

The Bonny Foundation provides resources and training in the therapeutic use of the arts for professional music therapists, related health professionals, and the general public.

Bread & Roses
78 Throckmorton Ave.
Mill Valley, CA 94941
Tel: (415) 381-0320
Fax: (415) 381-0323
E-mail: breadros@ricochet.net
Website: http://www.breadandroses.com

Bread & Roses is dedicated to uplifting the human spirit by providing free, live, quality entertainment to people who live in institutions or are otherwise isolated from society. Their performances promote wellness through the healing power of the performing arts. They also seek to create a social awareness of people who are isolated, and to encourage the development of similar organizations in other communities.

Center for Media Literacy
4727 Wilshire Blvd., Suite 403
Los Angeles, CA 90010
Tel: (800) 226-9494 or (213) 931-4177
Fax: (213) 931-4474
E-mail: cml@medialit.org
Website: http://www.medialit.org

An educational and membership organization that develops projects and materials to promote critical thinking about the media. The center's clearinghouse offers books, videos, and teaching materials for use in schools, parent education, community centers, or for any group interested in the media literacy movement.

The Moving Center
P.O. Box 2034
Red Bank, NJ 07701
Tel: (973) 642-1979
Fax: (973) 621-2185
Website: http://www.ravenrecording.com

Author and workshop leader Gabriel Roth has devoted her life to exploring and communicating the language of primal movement, ecstatic experience, and the journey of the soul. Contact for Roth's workshops.

Music for People

P.O. Box 397
Goshen, CT 06756
Tel: (860) 491-4511
Fax: (860) 491-4513
E-mail: davidcello@aol.com

Music for People promotes self-expression through music and improvisation. Founded by cellist and improvisor David Darling, their philosophy states that music is a natural creative expression available to everyone.

Music Therapists for Peace

P.O. Box 743, Cathedral Station
New York, NY 10025
Tel: (212) 865-6895
Call New York office for groups in other countries.
E-mail: boxill@is3.nyu.edu
Website: http://pages.nyu.edu/~boxill/mtp.html

Music Therapists for Peace, Inc. (MTP) was founded for the purpose of furthering peace on all levels of human existence through methods unique to the treatment modality of music therapy. It networks with music therapy professionals worldwide. MTP has also initiated a project called Students Against Violence Everywhere — S.A.V.E. — Through Music Therapy. S.A.V.E. is designed to reduce violence in schools.

National Endowment for the Arts

1100 Pennsylvania Ave., N.W.
Washington, D.C. 20506
Tel: (202) 682-5400
Website: http://arts.endow.gov

The National Endowment for the Arts is an independent agency of the U.S. Government created by Congress to support the arts and to provide education and access to the arts for all Americans. Their mission is to foster the excellence, diversity, and vitality of the arts, and to broaden public access to the arts.

Peace Museum
314 W. Institute Place
Chicago, IL 60610
Tel: (312) 440-1860
E-mail: peacegrams@compuserve.com

The Peace Museum is an educational institution whose mission is to motivate children, teens, and adults to achieve creative solutions to the problem of violence. The museum fulfills this mission through exhibitions, educational programs, publications, and a collection of 10,000 artworks and artifacts on the history and practice of peace. The museum's work helps to sustain the legacy of global cooperation created through peace, civil rights, human rights, and social justice movements worldwide.

The Touchstone Center
141 E. 88th St.
New York, NY 10028
Tel: (212) 831-7717

An educational organization that has been a leader in creating interdisciplinary arts programs in public schools. Through their publications, artist residencies in schools, theater productions, exhibitions, workshops, and seminars, the center sustains the importance of the imaginative process as a means of deepening individual and collective understanding.

Tamalpa Institute
P.O. Box 794
Kentfield, CA 94914
Tel: (415) 457-8555
Fax: (415) 457-7960
E-mail: tamalpa@igc.org

The Tamalpa Institute teaches an integrative approach to movement, the expressive arts, and therapeutic models. The program prepares students to become certified practitioners in movement-based expressive arts therapy and is also ideal for individuals who wish to incorporate creative skills into their professional practices. This work can be applied to the fields of psychology, education, and health.

CHAPTER EIGHT:
Toward a More Unified, Compassionate Society

See Chapter Six Resource Guide for Goldman Environmental Prize.

Gail Bernice Holland is the editor of *Connections*, a magazine of the Institute of Noetic Sciences. A journalist for more than thirty years, she has worked on newspapers and magazines in both Britain and the United States, and was a staff feature writer for the *San Francisco Examiner*. She has also worked in the movie industry. Her honors include the California State Bar Sigma Delta Chi Press Award for "outstanding achievement by an editorial worker in reporting and interpreting the administration of justice in California." Holland is the author of *For Sasha, with Love: An Alzheimer's Crusade* (Dembner, 1985), a book about the challenges of caring for those with Alzheimer's disease. She lives in the San Francisco Bay Area.